GALAXY GATE

Volume I
THE HOLY UNIVERSE

by
Ann Ree Colton
and
Jonathan Murro

ANN REE COLTON FOUNDATION
Post Office Box 2057
Glendale, California 91209

First Edition
Vol. 1 ISBN: 0-917189-02-7
Set of 2 Vols. ISBN: 0-917189-01-9
Library of Congress Catalog Card Number: 84-70851

For information regarding the writings and teachings
of Ann Ree Colton and Jonathan Murro,
write:

Ann Ree Colton Foundation
336 West Colorado Street
Post Office Box 2057
Glendale, California 91209
Telephone: (818) 244-0113

Printed in the United States of America
by DeVorss & Company, California

CONTENTS

Charts by Ann Ree Colton

Paintings by Ann Ree Colton

Charts by Jonathan Murro

FOREWORD

I have written all of my books out of the Great Unconscious or *Purusha*. My ego has not been involved in the writing of my books. I have offered all of my books as a gift and a service to all souls rising as suns in the expansion of their soul-powers.

Galaxy Gate shows the reality of the Hierarchs and man as a potential Hierarch. Men must bring forth their Virtue-Light. They must give birth to another degree of Conscience, which will move them forward into the Space Age or Interterrestrial pioneering and discovering.

The soul of man must move equal to his discovering principle. This inventive and intuitive attribute can be given only through Heavenly-directing processes of light uniting with Spirit Eternal in the minds of men.

The religious heart and the Galaxies are how one knows Universal God. Worship of God and union with His Reality are greater than a million telescopes or surveying methods, for by Universal and Cosmos intuition man experiences God as the One in Galaxy, in eternity, in stars and in planets.

The purpose of writing this book is to make one aware of the conjoining forces within the Intelligible energies supporting the Universe.

—A. R. C.

1

THIS, OUR EARTH

When the first Archangel spoke into etheric man before man took a coat of skin, it was said to him: "I give you now inner-parts wisdom containing all of the laws of creation and procreation. I share with you the knowledge of the hierarchy state of the divine being you are, and of the becoming for the sake of the Universal rather than the self."

The second Archangel said unto man on his taking a coat of skin: "I give you the Archetypal Knowledge of will and choice. By this Tree of Knowledge shall you become a hierarch-creator of many states of consciousness, whereby you learn your apprentice-skills.

"On taking your coat of skin, I am giving you the true hierarchy vehicle, which is divided into two: Time and Space. Through Time you will create, limited by choice. You will through right choosing master Space; and in the mastery of Space, you will know your sister stars, your planets, your sun and your moons.

"I will give to you, as one of the gifts of Timing, Cycles by which your knowledge is maintained and utilized. I will give unto you waking and sleep and death as the knowledgeable precincts of development. These three must be known by you with an aware and erect consciousness before you can become aware of the velocities of the energy impregnating and filling Space.

"Time is of the essence of your hierarchy mastery. Space is of the essence of your creating and extending as a consciousness being for this, our Earth."

PURE SPIRIT

> *Wherever you turn, you will find Me, for I am*
>   *there.*
> *In the midst of everything, I am the One.*
> *In the Time, I am the hour, the moment and the*
>   *second.*
> *In the Space, I am the breath.*
>
> *I am love.*
> *I am the life.*
> *I am the light.*
> *And I am the Will as Spirit in all.*
>
> *I am the Omnipresence within the conscience.*
> *I am the Omniscience in the light.*
> *I am the Omnipotence in the will.*
>
> *Who doeth My Will without love will fail.*
> *He who doeth My works without truth will fall.*
> *He who liveth in My breath without reverence for*
>   *life will die.*
> *He who hateth My light will live in eternal*
>   *darkness.*
>
> *To the blind, to the maimed, to the afflicted, I say*
>   *to you:* Love.
> *You will find Me where love is.*
> *I am the Spirit of Love,*
>   *the Spirit of Truth,*
>   *the Spirit of Living.*
> *I am the Power.*

God is the Center. His Universe is an expanding and contracting Universe. He expands His Spirit in a circle. He returns to His Center and re-spiritualizes His Universe after periods or intervals of rest. His whole Creation is based upon Expansion, Contraction, Compression.

Spirit is Power. Spirit as Power progresses and regresses and compresses. This is the Law of the Three within the Spirit of God. That which compresses has within its nature both expansion and contraction. So is the nature of God as Spirit in man and in His Universe, His Galaxies, His Stars and His Eternities.

All is Spirit. Time in the consciousness of man functions in rhythmic and periodical cycles as extensions of Spirit.

Matter as expansion of God is Energy geometrized to time-limit flexibilities within cause and effect. In returning to the Center or Spirit, matter undergoes contraction or return into Pure Spirit.

Pure Spirit—which is God as the Center or Motivator of will, life, light and love—geometrizes itself into expression as form. Form is energy in mass quickened by Pure Spirit; animated by Pure Spirit as Will of God.

Life as Pure Spirit is functional in form as breath, mind—sentient and conscious. Light as Pure Spirit in matter or form is realization as Pure Spirit. Realization is Creation within the Spirit of Creation.

Love in form is that which is aware of Pure Spirit as constant and sustaining; perfection unlimited, infinite; ever-creating; manifesting as will, life, light, love.

There are different states of compression in the geometrized Spirit represented as man with consciousness. Compression occurs when man experiences realization, for he has returned to Pure Spirit as a knowing, conscious being. Each thought containing Illumination and Revelation is a moment of compressed union with God.

At death, there is a time element of compressed extension into the state of death. From the time of death to the next birth, one exists in a soul-compressed state of union with God as Pure Spirit.

All is Pure Spirit in different degrees. There is no death in Pure Spirit. In *all* existence — Cosmos, Cosmic and material — Pure Spirit is the deathless element which sends its Spirit and calls it into its Center. This is the logistics by which Eternals create and recreate — the Universal Logistics which have no variance; for Eternal Spirit as perfection is Eternal, eternally creating as Birth, Expansion; as Death, Contraction; as Quiescence, Compression.

The period of Pure Spirit Quiescence correlates to the Day of the Sabbath in which man through worship and prayer communes with Pure Spirit as Quiescence. There are Rest resurgences in which man as creator with mind must have intervals of respite, that he may receive the creative impulses of the mind on renewed spirals of enterprising waves of Creation.

> *God is a Spirit: and they that worship him must worship him in spirit and in truth.*
>   *—St. John 4:24*

The encounter with the Spirit of God is a Cosmos Encounter. A seeker knowing not what he seeks lives in the partial and the biased. A seeker daring to encounter Eternal Spirit opens his mind to Cosmos hearing, seeing and knowing.

God works with the Cosmos Patience. Man must learn to work with the Cosmos Patience. *"In your patience possess ye your souls."* (St. Luke 21:19)

In union with the Cosmos Spirit, one thinks within an eternity system and Eternal System. When one once reaches this union, the bias of eternity transenergizes into an Eternal Vision. This Vision is patient, seeing the Plan and the Scheme of God in milleniums rather than in finite cycles and days.

When man offends the Union Principle of oneness with
God, he turns back the clock of evolution and evolvement.
When a whole eternity system becomes godless in consciousness, the result is anomaly in procreation, in consciousness; the planetary system enters into a stage of death
and dying, for that which is God as Consciousness is the Diamond of Incentive in all eternity systems.

Belief in God is essential to this eternity system in which
man dwells, for without it man becomes lower than the
animals and beasts of the earth. Presently, it is by God-belief
that God is able to manifest through His Son, the Christ. The
many lands and countries now no longer believing in God —
and living in the godless state — are killing the incentive trans-
missions through which God flows into the consciousness of
man.

To be godless to the True Self is desolation and separation.
To be godless en masse is to be below the vibrational keynote
of the eternity system in which one dwells.

Calamities come to the world when men link themselves
with godless ideas, godless beliefs and godless actions. Nature
herself responds to love and retreats from the acids of hate
and separation. The animals and all of their species respond
to God through joy of life.

The soul is a buoyancy-vehicle of supernatural energy. It
is the receptive vehicle which contains within its nature the
direct orders for order in this eternity system and in all other
eternity systems of the past and of the future. These orders
have four aspects called *Fiats*. The four Fiats are Will, Life,
Light and Love. The Fiats function directly through the inherent nature of existence and life, conscious and unconscious, in all worlds.

God the One — the Spirit in All — is the Will, the Life, the
Light, the Love. The Spirit of God cannot be moved: He *is*
Will, Life, Light, Love. Man is empowered to fulfill the four
Fiats as ordained within the Spirit of God.

The True Self, by its very nature, lives within the four Fiat-states of becoming, existence and being. The soul, in its buoyancy, works as a pulsating field for the four Fiats. By the virtue of these, the Higher Self sends forth its Eternal Knowing. This Knowing is differentiated into ego-experience in many states of willing, in many paths of life incarnating, in many and varied ways of learning and knowing, and in many versatile ways of loving. All of these are within the Will, the Life, the Light and the Love of God.

God projected from His Spirit the Christ—the only begotten Son—which is the Light.

God as Spirit projected from His Spirit the Fathers, Who are the creators within the *Life*. The Life of the Spirit is in the Fathers where the Archetypal Images in the use of forming and making gave the Life, which is Man, and all creatures having life, sentient and conscious.

God as Spirit gave the Holy Ghost and the functioning of the Holy Spirit, which is the Esse and Spirit of Truth, to maintain the original truths in Law and order upholding the creative formats of Spirit or God.

God as Love manifested through Jesus, giving to mankind the Son of Man made wholly and completely as a perfected Image. Jesus, as Christ Jesus, manifested the Son-of-God powers in the world as Spirit. Man, as a soul of pure Spirit, is deathless, destined to reincarnate until perfection in the spirit of the likeness of Jesus is fulfilled in this Earth.

God, as Love in man, functions as Union, as Happiness, as Bliss, as Peace. God, as the Will in man, generates choice and action. God, as Spirit in the *life* of man, activates functioning as living. God, as the Spirit of Truth in man, functions as *Law*, correcting, reproving, revealing.

Consciousness comes to birth in all eternity systems through which God as Omnipresence manifests Himself as the One Spirit. God, as Spirit, functions in all eternity systems or solar systems as Quickening through the four Fiat Spirit-attributes. All who experience God-Realization must incorporate the four Great Fiats.

God is not in the possession of any one religion, creed, doctrine or dogma. He who thinks of God as being his possession uses the organization principle of his own or separative creation to function as *ego*.

Soul absent from God by past sinful and willful omissions produces a godless state. All suffering comes from absence from God or Spirit. All healing begins in Spirit and ends in the Spiritual. He who has been healed once through faith in God as Spirit, Eternal, Infinite, has remembrance of God, and will thirst to return to God through Realization.

Throughout the ages, the Will of God has imprinted itself upon the Earth, and the Life of God has moved without ceasing in all forms of sentience, non-sentience, and also in varying ways of consciousness. The Love of God is that which saves, succors, secures, heals, blesses, unites, softens, blends—giving hope, giving peace, giving purpose.

God as Life is ever-present as Omnipresence. God, as Omnipresence, as Light in the soul of man, is obtained through His only begotten Son, the Christ. Wherever Light is, the Omnipresence of God and the Presence of His Son are seen. In the Godly, it is seen in the Intelligible. In those less Godly, it is seen as the unintelligent.

As the five senses work for each other, the four Fiats also work together. If any one of the Earth has in his existing prototypal pattern more or excess of the Will Fiat than any of the other Fiats, he will suffer in both the body and the mind. Existence will be difficult for him in Earth and in Heaven.

If anyone has a tendency to lean more upon the Life Fiat than any of the other Fiats, he will see life as a struggle for survival. He will be over-competitive; he will be possessive, jealous. In this modern time, he will be inclined toward the humanistic, believing in the law of man as creator rather than the Life of God as Creation.

If anyone has single dependency upon the Light Fiat, he will be intellectually dependent upon his senses rather than upon the Intelligible Purusha, which is centered in Buddhi or the Informing Principle.

If anyone has his imaging processes fixed upon those whom he personally loves with possessive dependencies, he will enter into the discipline-trials of separateness and loneliness.

All of the four Fiats are offered to man that he may become a whole being while living in the Earth in the spirit of goodness. One should pray to be not dependent upon any one Fiat, but to ask for the blessing of the fourfold comprehension supporting the divine order of existence and of consciousness.

The soul duplicates and activates the Will of God, the Life of God, the Light of God and the Love of God according to the order of God. By this, God keeps His order perpetually active in every function of His Universes and worlds.

He who has seen a Black Hole has seen the ending of a cluster of eternity systems where Spirit as order indraws itself to create a new beginning, a new phase of Creation. Whoever encounters by seership or by telescopes a White-Hole beginning of a new cycle of Creation learns that there is no ending in Creation, but only that which men call order and Time and Space used by God to manifest His Face or Spirit in all worlds, all kingdoms, all journeys.

The soul is a unit of energy, a deathless, indestructible unit of the Spirit of God, housing the Eternal Self, which is a son of God. Man, as a son of man, must learn that he is innately a son of God. There are periods in time when the Spirit of God calls to His sons an order to "Return, ye sons of God."

THE POWER OF GOODNESS

> *Oh how great is thy goodness, which thou hast laid up for them that fear thee; which thou hast wrought for them that trust in thee before the sons of men!*
>
> *—Psalm 31:19*

This eternity system (solar system) is a goodness system. Men are in this Earth to receive and to manifest goodness. That which is good in man is *"the peace of God, which passeth all understanding." (Philippians 4:7)* Goodness will ultimately be meekness, that man may inherit the Earth as a hierarchy creator for God.

Having been begotten in the very heart of Spirit as Love, man experiences love first as goodness in an eternity system set upon the axis-pole of duality. By victory over darkness through good shall man resurrect the axis-pole of the Earth, and move it into the vibration of a greater consciousness, which is of the Christ.

God loved this world, and He gave to it the Christ. The Christ Spirit as Light concentrates the Ray of His Spirit—Light—upon the axis-pole of the Earth, that men may hasten to become good and to overthrow evil, darkness, unknowing and separation.

God is the Power. Man comes into fullness as an authority-vehicle for God when he begins to live for good.

Goodness as the Esse, by the very nature of the spirit of good, overcomes evil. Good, having no self-aggressions, is beyond the reach of evil.

Evil suffers in its futility on being exposed to true and pure good. Evil is transenergized by good, or the energies in evil are transformed into peace by that which is the likeness of God in the spirit of good.

Victory over evil produces virtue, which gives fresh renewals of rationality and of inspiration. Goodness lacking the transfusions of virtue becomes a dry functioning for self-indulgence through the ego.

In all religions, goodness must undergo periods of Initiation whereby one's goodness is tested. When the soul-energy in a religious body is apathetic or *tamas*, it is not a coherent body. A coherent body of worshippers attends a worship service contributing to the inquiry or desire to know, to understand, and thus gives to the priest or minister a way on which his own cognizance may flow into the expectations of those attending.

It is the work of the shepherd, minister or teacher to set goals for the sheep as to how they should worship and what worship truly means. A coherent worship-body produces a sheath of cognizance. When cognizance is coordinated, it provides a living body through which the Omnipresence of God lifts all, blesses all, heals all.

If one does not have love in the mind, intelligence cannot live. An inquiring intelligence without love turns to intellectual dependency.

Intellect is self-made by man as an individual. Intelligence is the innate birthright of man given to him by God.

There must be always the intuitive heart, knowing that one is sent of God to the world. If one degrades his intelligence which stems from the heart by failing to grow in his emotions, he turns to the worship of his own intellect rather than to the worship of God through his innate intelligence or *knowing*.

Intellect is seasonal, therefore perishable. Intelligence is eternal, drawing its eternality from the wellsprings of Spirit and spiritual love.

An enlarged soul-space is an enlarged enlightenment as to where one is going and from whence he has come. With the coming of the Christ in Jesus, those with enlarged soul-enlightenment heard and responded to this call. No one in the Earth can stand between Jesus and His goodness, for God would use Him as His Son, that His work and Will might be done in this Earth and in Heaven.

> *Wherefore also we pray always for you, that our God would count you worthy of this calling, and fulfill all the good pleasure of his goodness, and the world of faith with power: That the name of our Lord Jesus Christ may be glorified in you, and ye in him, according to the grace of our God and the Lord Jesus Christ.*
> *—2 Thessalonians 1:11,12*

ULTIMATE VIRTUE

The Name of God holds together all Galaxies.

The whole state of Cosmos is Virtue—exquisite Virtue. The Galaxy Universe is balanced by the central heliocentric Virtue. Each Galaxy contains one heliocentric Virtue-particle or Divine Atom, which is the commanding pole for the polarities within each Galaxy.

A virtue is one of the Ultimates of God; it is an Eternal Ultimate. An Ultimate is a tool for soul-destiny, assuring man that he is a creator in the physical world sent forth as a soul from Eternal God.

A virtue can appear in the world as a Face of God, for when one witnesses virtue, he has seen the Presence of God. Through virtue, man lives in patience with the world. Through virtue, man understands Time and Space as a part of the skills of his creating.

A virtue is a perfected asset used by man to reveal his own purpose and to fulfill the Ultimate Plan as destined of God.

God planted the Ultimate-Virtue system in man so that man would not fall into oblivion as a soul.

The most wholesome beauty is virtue-beauty. Virtue-beauty is the beauty of the soul-emergence into the whole of life, producing a whole person.

Virtue-beauty is centered in mortal and immortal goodness shining forth upon the countenance, the movements of the body, and the expression of the individual. The deep, sweet memories of a beloved face, of a beloved deed, passed on from a pure soul, leave the undying mark of good which all crave, desire, and hope for.

The lamp of grace keeps alive virtue-beauty. It spreads as a hope and a blessing upon everyone and everything. Anyone containing any form of conceit or inflation of ego is devoid of virtue-beauty.

The virtues are not gained unless one has the disciplines. *Sadhana* means discipline. Discipline leads to right virtue and to right grace.

The discipline of a former life builds the virtue for the present life. The virtue of the present builds the grace for the next life. These are the three infallibles of Salvation.

In the life of grace, the cycle renews; one takes his discipline again on a higher spiral, assisted by grace. From this rhythm in Salvation comes the Solar Initiate, the Androgynous Being free of Time and Space; the Phoenix Bird beyond delusion. With the four faces of the Dharma, the Fiats, he looks out of the Galaxy Gate and is at home in the Universe.

Every solar system, by its own unique mathematical process, works to produce Virtue. This virtue is of a quality and nature relating to the initiations of fulfillment in service to Creation, to God.

The total Universe exists in a stabilized Constant of Virtue. One never loses the stability morality-virtue inherent in the soul. As one advances more and more through the use of this morality in other eternity systems, the responsibility is greater; for through awareness and learning, the need for virtue increases.

The total Universe is a stabilized morality system. Non-virtue is perishable in this system. Non-virtue, by its own instability, must die or be eliminated by the Constant as Virtue in the total Universe.

The Constant of God is the Virtue. He who lives in the Constant of God creates for God with perfection.

In each eternity or solar system where consciousness is active, one learns what virtues are necessary, and he incorporates this learning into his own consciousness. Those who live in a duality system must contend always with the *other*; one learns by comparison and analysis.

Until the coming of Jesus, man in this Earth had no way to compare his own morality and virtue with the state of consciousness in other eternity systems. From Jesus, one learns that he is Universal in his own nature, that he is inherently virtuous. This knowledge makes him a part of the wisdom and intelligible communications uniting all eternity systems. No longer identifying himself as virtue being singly of his own nature, he will live within the continuing Constant of God in the Universal Whole. It is this clean virtue of the Constant Universal that keeps the Universe stable within its Archetypal System of Time and Space, Here and There, Now and Forever.

All men are Cosmos souls eternally scheduled for many cosmic journeys or sojourns in this Earth and in many other eternity systems to come. Souls, as men in Earth, are here by Divine Plan within an unceasing Divine Order.

He who makes himself illegitimate is a bastard by his own incrimination. He who believes not in God has made himself an outcast fragment. To be wrapped in the blanket of genetic limitation devoid of soul-expansion is to be little more than an insect, an animal, a tree or a stone.

It is fallacy to believe that one can manage this Earth's system by oneself. It is the work of man to go to the atom and to find its spiritual rate of vibration, that he may step out of and beyond the insidious inferences of limited action.

Gravity-bound man is limited by one thing: Disbelief in God. Purusha-man or Infinite-man united with the core of Galaxy-relatings is free, unlimited, unbound, deathless.

LOGIC AND VIRTUE

Love is the supporting element for every virtue.

Logic is the Logos of the mind. Logic is the higher rationale through which man links himself to Creation.

Attentiveness and concentration-exercises build logic. The closer one comes to the higher logic, the more he must detach himself from the heated aspects of the lower mind.

Intuition furnishes logic of a higher order. True and pure logic is a higher-mind vehicle. Virtue is a will vehicle. Intuition is a soul vehicle. All are dependent upon the Soul. Each functions in its individual way, but is interrelated with the others, even as the senses are separate but work together.

The senses are dependent upon the desire; virtue and logic are dependent upon the soul. Pure desire is a necessity to free the virtues. The more selfless the desire, the greater the power of the virtue.

The virtue powers are Kingdom-powers. The heart and core of virtue is *selfless goodness*. This is the goodness Jesus spoke of as contained by the Father in Heaven.

The living virtue is to be found in the Agape. He who passes on the living virtue in his service to God is in the Word of God; *he is the Word of God made flesh.*

Man is in the Earth to master man-to-man vibrations. The man-vibrations animate; the God-Vibrations radiate and emanate. There can be no separation from God, for God is the All, the One.

Self-complacency produces pseudo-virtues. A person who follows a few rules by complying with acceptable conduct and thinks himself to be filled with virtues is in the state of pseudo-virtue. Such virtue is not accounted in Heaven as grace.

One's own Archetypal Image is the Image of God within himself. Each life is given to one that he may reclaim the virtues gained in former lives and use them to bring forth latent virtues which are potential within the Archetype or Image of God within him.

If a person does not have spontaneity-powers or quick thinking, he is not close to his gifts. Spontaneity is the creativity aspect which surges upward from the gifts. All gifts are rooted in virtues earned in past lives.

One of the finest of Earth-earned virtues is the acceptance of training, discipline and learning. The Father gives to every one the right to seal the door where evil dwells.

Repentance prevents the *second death. "He that overcometh shall not be hurt of the second death." (Revelation 2:11)*

Every virtue-act conceals a master virtue. Concealed within Repentance is Humility. Without humility, one cannot sustain repentance, for the dark agencies loose in the world are seeking constantly to render a blow to his repentance, testing it against the solid rock of Humility.

The soul cannot be restored without humility. Every particle of arrogance must be mastered before the soul can shine as a sun in its full splendor, restoring that which was lost or fallen or dark.

Modesty is the first virtue of the will. Modesty is that which takes one to the door of Humility. Humility means surrender, total surrender to God.

. . . be clothed with humility: for God resisteth the proud, and giveth grace to the humble. Humble yourselves therefore under the mighty hand of God, that he may exalt you in due time.

—1 Peter 5:5,6

VIRTUE-ENERGY

And he said unto her, Daughter, thy faith hath made thee whole; go in peace, and be whole of thy plague.

—St. Mark 5:34

In Jesus, Virtue was the accumulated bank account or reservoir for healing. The woman healed of the issue of blood (St. Mark 5:25–35) contacted this Virtue in Jesus by touching His garment with absolute faith.

If the one being healed receives the Passing of the Virtue, the Virtue healing-power must in turn be passed on by the one who has received the healing. If one does not voice his gratitude for being healed, the virtue-power within his healing is made static. The Ethic of Transmission was fulfilled when the woman healed of the issue of blood by the Virtue in Jesus made testimony of her healing—and the virtue-strength in Jesus was recovered.

Virtue is a tangible substance emanating from the one containing Virtue. This substance permeates and pervades environments, clothing, objects.

Pervading virtue in holy relics also manifests as healing miracles. The handkerchiefs of Saint Paul were passed on to the faithful, where the holy aromas of his virtue produced miraculous healing.

Jesus transmitted or passed His Virtue onto Saint Paul, opening the soul-power virtue of Paul. This Virtue of Jesus is passed onto him who is faithful in soul and in works.

And the whole multitude sought to touch Him:
for there went virtue out of Him, and healed them
all.

—*St. Luke 6:19*

This Eternity System is seeking to become a *Virtue* Eternity System. All are working to obtain Virtue. Men will walk the Path of Sweet Virtue built in the castle of the soul and the spirit.

When the last aeon of this eternity system has finished its course, the Sun or Solar Vortex will be a Celestial Diamond in the starry lights of Celestial Perfection.

Virtues are Heavenly will-attributes in man. For every Eternal Atom there is a Virtue.

A virtue is not illumined unless it has at its roots God as Spirit. All have latent virtues awaiting to be quickened. Virtues come to the birth state of illumination through the desire to give and to serve.

Virtue gives off life-giving energy. Virtue flow of energy is soul-energy acting as life-force energy in the blood. This life-force energy is supported by the etheric body of Jesus.

The virtue-energy is in the higher etheric body. When virtue is misused, virtue-energy flow is depleted in the etheric body.

A mediative healer can be drained of his life-force energies when he is taken unawares or imposed upon by those seeking to use his healing for non-virtuous acts.

One is the descendant of both his virtue-grace and his dark karma.

A man should keep the virtue of his seed as he would keep the purity of the oil in the lamp within the sanctuary. A woman should keep the chastity-virtue of her birthing-power pure and undefiled, that she may contain in her womb pure souls sent from God.

Kindness has never been passed on through the genes; it

is passed on through the Archetypal soul-power. Kindness is one of the diamond-virtues.

The six diamond-virtues are kindness, trust, enthusiasm, willingness, truth and youthful naivete. A person can be old in years but still have a youthful naivete.

The six diamond-virtues are a part of the Archetypal Light. The soul setting out to Earth-birth with these six diamond points of grace renews and relives happily within the life-stream of mankind. Earth-joy is known by those having the six diamond-virtues. Such joy is contagious, hopeful, happy.

The Cosmos Virtue in the sky makes it possible for a bird to fly and to migrate.

GALAXY-GATE PLANETS

There is one glory of the sun, and another glory of the moon, and another glory of the stars: for one star differeth from another star in glory.
—1 Corinthians 15:41

Man is incubated in the Galaxies; he is nursed in the Sun; he is schooled by the Planets; and he is utilized in an Earth System for God as a creator through his union with the Cosmos.

The Galaxy Gate concerns the encounter with the Intelligible Omnipresence centered in the total Universe, in command of all Creation. From the world of the atom to the world of man as consciousness, Omnipresence is in command and is present in all functions and actions.

By looking toward the three planets closest to the Galaxy Gate—Uranus, Neptune and Pluto—one can know where he is, why he is, and where he is going. These three far-out planets control, identify and determine the hierarchy destiny for man — that is, his inward God-design, which is written in the stars and functioning through the planets upon the higher etheric bodies of man.

When man became aware of Uranus (1781), Neptune (1846), and Pluto (1930), the Galaxy Gate opened; the minds of men, inventions, individuality, all received directly the downpouring of Galaxy-wisdoms and revelation. During the present period, there are great changes in the Earth itself regarding man and his soul- and mind-freedoms. In this, he comes closer to God and God-Realization. He becomes a universal being rather than an earthling dependent upon one solar system. He becomes a child of the Universe, a companion to communicable planetary systems in affinity to his own Sun or Solar System.

The energy-processes of the flow of Galaxy moved men beyond the enclosures of primal developments. Thus, in the years 1781, 1846 and 1930, men of the Earth began to express Self-Genesis rather than Family-Genesis and Tribal-Genesis.

The Self-Genesis Age began to function as consciousness in the mind of man in the year of 1930. Man then became aware of himself as a Self-Genesis expression. Individual expression and individuality or the self demanded recognition.

The United States of America is a Galaxy-Gate cradle for the birth to Self-Genesis in the Earth.

1776. United States became a nation.

1781. Discovery of Uranus.

1812-1815. War of 1812.

1846. Discovery of Neptune.

1861-1865. Civil War. Freeing of the Slaves.

1929-1939. Great Depression.

1930. Discovery of Pluto

1939-1945. World War II.

The most realistic and open expression for Self-Genesis occurred in the year of 1930. The work begun by Uranus in 1781 and the following energy-processes of Neptune in 1846 were culminated by Pluto to produce a complete reformation in human consciousness, and thus man became fully charged with individualization as an ego in his own right.

Since the year of 1930, men have been in constant states of war and conflict to assert their rights as individuals. The open Galaxy Gate pressures men to create; and, in creating through soul-expansion, men move forward toward God-Realization. In the great Archetypal Intervals, when the Galaxy Gate opens, men become self-makers, self-creators, using their Imaging Powers to manifest great and mighty things in the likeness of their Creator.

Every 248 years Pluto's orbit brings it inside the orbit of Neptune for a 20-year period. From 1979 to 1999, Neptune, rather than Pluto, will be the planet farthest from the Sun. During the 20-year cycle that Pluto is enclosed into the energy-spheres of Neptune, men will meet a master crisis which will culminate 100 years of Uranus rajasic stimulation. When the 20-year cycle has concluded, Pluto will function as a channeling revelator for knowledge heretofore inaccessible.

Pluto presently may be likened to a space satellite with a processing camera recording knowledge of the brother and sister eternity systems of this Eternity System. This knowledge is inaccessible through gross states of consciousness.

Pluto provides the germ-seeds for man's intuition and reach into the future. Its effect upon men works totally upon the subconscious minds of men and the collective consciousness of mankind.

When men seek to concern themselves solely with Earth identity as to evolvement, Pluto remains unawakened in their natures. When men reach out in wonder, in daring, in venture and in research, Pluto is stirred. The subconscious filters into the mind through intuitive processes of learning.

Pluto, a small terrain, is a mediator for man, a true awakener of soul-processes latent and potential. When the 20-years have concluded of Pluto's confinement within close proximity to Neptune, Pluto will produce the revelatory into the actualities of the physical. Men will truly begin the interterrestrial state; they will experience concrete and direct knowledge concerning their space companions of the Universe. Prophecies long nourished regarding man's potential as continuity, as imperishable, will be confirmed by actual acknowledgment and manifestation of a new world order directly affecting the consciousness of man.

In the brief period of one century, all of the inventive processes for the new era and time have been presented as tools for the coming interterrestrial age. These are the tools which will lead men into superhuman tasks of mind, soul and spirit.

Man must make a leap in conscience and in consciousness that he may be equal to the demands of the new era before him.

Many of the young now are being born in the Earth with interterrestrial expectations. Men who refuse to remove themselves from the tamas-inertias will be unprepared to teach and to lead such souls who are committed to the expansion of soul through Time and Space.

In this time, many souls who have indulged in gross sensuality and have fixed their minds upon the pleasure principle will remain laggard. Pleasure, as men think of it now, will by necessity be totally changed in that men will return to exact principle and thereby willingly and unwillingly walk toward the Path of Truth. Those who are unwilling will experience insensitive brutalities from institutions and bureaucracies. The present shaping of the continents and the nations in the human spirit foretells the state of the future. Each day man's loss of individuality as a soul and a spirit is indenting future grief and suffering.

Man presently is in a delirium of astral obnoxinity. He has

dared to profane his atmosphere given to him as a green pasture of stewardship.

The Great Unconscious is the *Purusha* or the Archetypal Knowledge. The Great Unconscious is opened by certain advanced souls who have the power to reach and to familiarize themselves with the coordinating and collective creating forces of the Universe. Those having this power bring soul-knowledge to men of the Earth before it is proven by science. These foreseeing-ones prepare men to receive soul-knowledge directly and to put it into action through events which appear seemingly out of nowhere, but which in reality function as a direct process of revelation and creation.

The collective Higher Unconscious is presently pouring down to mankind of the Earth heretofore unmanifested Archetypal Ideas providing the inspiration for the building of the new human race, a race with one foot on Earth and one foot on outer-space terrain.

Previously, man has been engaged in acreage, footage, miles. He now enters into spheres, by which he will venture into sister and brother planets, and move outward into Galaxy-experiencing through the Gate of Galaxy.

The collective subconscious of mankind is mottled with outpouring abscesses caused by offences in the trade-ethic of this time. Man has over-traded himself with Nature. He has out-smarted himself with science and technology. He has understaffed and misplaced himself religiously.

The danger of death to an Earth can be precipitated by masses of destroying minds that have failed God in themselves. Non-diligent prophets and spurious exploiters of human nature fail themselves as channels for God.

Animals follow the rules of survival, responding to the seasons and the cycles. Yet, upon them has been thrust man's oppression which has set up obstacles against their path of specie-evolution.

Within the next 100 years, thousands of species of the insect and animal kingdoms will be withdrawn from the Earth. With their going, man will lose many aspects in his own immunity or antibody system, as the correlated functioning of each creature below the chain of man's evolvement is a necessary support for man. When this immunity system is withdrawn, man will be exposed to conditions of the body in which he will have no recourse. No degree of technology or science will contain the answers for the diseases now coming upon man. These diseases, so interconnected with the processes of the mind of man, are beginning to appear in the minds of men; thinking of them as mental sicknesses, scientists and physicians are seeking to heal these conditions of the mind with drugs, with chemicals.

There is presently no preparation for these encounters, as total ignorance and blindness exist into the *why* of these happenings, and also the failure to see man's own responsibility for having set them into motion. In this boomerang process between greed of the eyes and permissiveness in the flesh, men are scourgers rather than stewards of their Holy Earth.

This Earth has been borne as a willing burden by the animal kingdom. The animal kingdom no longer can endure these repetitive pressures from the blind exploitation of the masses who care not for them, thinking only of how to devour and how to abuse them.

Every form of life in this Earth has meaning. And every form of life in this Earth is dependent upon all other forms of life. Only when man can realize this Earth is a starry field of Intelligible energies — every thing speaking to something else that it may live and grow — can he realize the wholeness of his soul in its meaning.

It is so sad to contemplate the waste of mind, of intelligence, or reasonable cognizant knowing. It is so terrible that men refuse to rise beyond subhuman exploration.

The Earth itself is the backdrop or scene for man's spiritual destiny in Earth, yet men continue blindly on, destroying, bruising, forcing. He who seeks to suffocate this Earth dies.

Man, in his ego-estimation of his own capacity, is moving in a revolving door of existence, or a merry-go-round of static confusion. The most profound dunce—if a dunce can be profound—is man.

This beautiful Earth. It is longing to give us birth. This beautiful Nature is longing to see man feeding each hungry creature. This blessed Earth spurns not any man. This blessed Earth. This Earth.

All men are Moon-cradled in an Earth which is living within the Soul of the Sun. One must master first the Moon forces in his own nature to become a Sun Initiate.

Astrology, as it presently exists, is to be made obsolete by astronomy's discoveries, in that it will be brought forward into a Cosmos scale of divining or knowing. The basic, dependable truths within astrology will be retained. Astrology will no longer use the same rules by which it takes upon itself the total interpretation of human affairs.

Science will prove that man is influenced by other eternity systems having one or more Suns and by the multiplicity of Moons influencing the lunar system of the Earth and its influence upon the glandular and emotional systems of man. The fixed stars in the twelve constellations also will be used as a take-off point through which men will come to understand the true creative fiats for their shaping and forming and for temperament and character propensities. These observations are to be used by scientific, universal astronomers and astrologists.

Until now, the growth of the mind of man has been stunted by the evolutionary beliefs of the forming and shaping of man being specifically interpreted as proceeding from the animal kingdom. Cosmos science through astronomy will reveal man's true origins.

The computer sciences will exceed the telescope and take men into the Infinite rather than anchor them into the finite. The computer, the laser and other degrees of energy will open to man the true and manifold energy-processes of this, our Universe. Man will no longer say "Our solar system," but will speak of "Our Universal System."

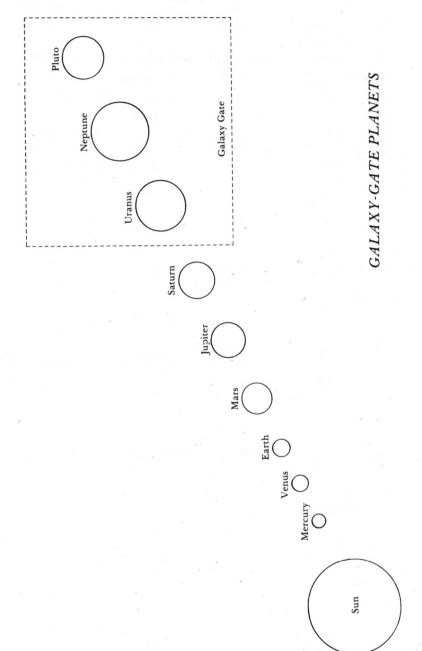

GALAXY-GATE PLANETS

UNIVERSE

The beginning of the universe is the mother of all things.
— Lao Tzu, 604-531 B.C.

Just as light is diffused from a fire which is confined to one spot, so is this whole universe the diffused energy of the supreme Brahman.
— *Visnu, Puranas*, c. 500 B.C.

This vast universe is a wheel. Upon it are all creatures that are subject to birth, death, and rebirth. Round and round it turns, and never stops. It is the wheel of Brahman.
— *Svetasvatara Upanishad*, before 400 B.C.

When we once understand that the universe is a great smelting-pot, and the Creator a great founder, where can we go that will not be right?
— Chuang-Tzu, 4th Century B.C.

As large as the universe outside, even so large is the universe within the lotus of the heart. Within it are heaven and the earth, the sun, the moon, the lightning, and all the stars. What is in the macrocosm is in this microcosm.
— The Upanishads

Since we preconceive by an indubitable notion that He (God) is a living being and . . . that there is nothing in all nature superior to Him, I do not see that anything can be more consistent . . . than to attribute life and divinity to the universe.
— Cicero, 44 B.C.

The whole universe together participates in the divine goodness more perfectly, and represents it better than any single creature whatever.
— St. Thomas Aquinas, 1272

The whole universe is but the footprint of the divine goodness.
— Dante, c. 1300

2

THE HOLY UNIVERSE

I am the door.
—St. John 10:9

Dedicated to the Lord Jesus as the Door to man's understanding the Universe.

Reverent gratitude to my beloved Teacher, Ann Ree Colton, who has inspired me to look at God's Universe through the Telescope of Prayer and Meditative Love.

Gratitude to the dedicated men and women of Science who are discovering priceless Truths regarding the Sun, the Moon, the Planets, the Stars and the Galaxies.

My portion of sharing in this book is based upon my gratitude for the wisdom of the ancients, the brilliance of modern-day astronomers, and the Scriptural promises of spiritual knowledge that comes through union with God.

Each scientific discovery about the wonders of Space contributes to the growth of the minds of men. When these discoveries are accompanied by a deep love for the Creator, the heart as well as the mind becomes involved in a rapturous closeness with the Cosmos.

Since 1952, Ann Ree Colton has taught me many truths regarding man's past, present and future. Especially have I come to value her inspired teaching about the important role being played by Jesus as the Mediator between man and God, man and the Universe.

"The Kingdom of God is within you." (St. Luke 17:21) The outer or visible Universe challenges the minds of men to investigate and to comprehend its beauty and design. Many individuals also feel compelled to learn about the beauty and design of the Inner Kingdom to which Jesus referred. When the Outer Universe and the Inner Kingdom become as one in one's heart and mind, he has attained a high degree of Enlightenment. I pray that this book will inspire sincere Truth-seekers to perceive the Hand of God creating the Inner and the Outer as One Holy Creation.

> *Virtue is the nature of God.*
> *Virtue is the nature of the Universe.*
>
> *Law is the nature of God.*
> *Law is the nature of the Universe.*
>
> *Love is the nature of God.*
> *Love is the nature of the Universe.*
>
> *Therefore, O devotee, if you would unite*
> *with God and His Universe, learn of Virtue,*
> *Law and Love.*

HERITAGE OF GALAXY KNOWLEDGE

> There is nothing so far removed from us as to be beyond our reach or so hidden that we cannot discover it.
>
> — Descartes

And with an awful, dreadful list,
Toward other galaxies unknown,
Ponderously turns the Milky Way.

—Boris Pasternak

• The first theory of the telescope was introduced by Johannes Kepler (1571-1630).

My greatest desire is that I may perceive the God whom I find everywhere in the external world, in like manner also within and inside myself.

—Kepler

• Galileo Galilei (1564-1642) built a telescope in 1609. His research increased mankind's range of perception from 6,000 stars seen with the naked eye to 50,000 stars observed through the telescope.

When I consider how many and how great mysteries men have understood, discovered, and contrived, I very plainly know and understand the mind of man to be one of the works of God, yea, one of the most excellent.

—Galileo

• Immanuel Kant (1724-1804) was the first to theorize the existence of galaxies, calling them "island universes" of stars.

Two things fill me with constantly increasing admiration and awe, the longer and more earnestly I reflect on them: *the starry heavens without and the moral law within*.

—Kant

• William Herschel (1738-1822) determined the shape of the Milky Way Galaxy. He discovered the planet Uranus in 1781, and also plotted the path of the Sun through Space.

• Vesto Melvin Slipher (1875-1969) discovered in 1913 that about a dozen galaxies in the vicinity of the Milky Way were moving away from the Earth at very high speeds, ranging up to two million miles per hour.

• In 1917 Albert Einstein (1879-1955) published his equations of general relativity. William de Sitter (1872-1934), a Dutch astronomer, predicted an expanding Universe. Arthur Eddington (1882-1944), an English astronomer, and Edwin Hubble (1889-1953), an American astronomer, contributed to the knowledge of an expanding Universe with outward moving galaxies.

> In the mystic sense of the creation around us, in the expression of art, in a yearning towards God, the soul grows upward and finds fulfillment of something implanted in its nature.
>
> — A. Eddington

> The most beautiful thing we can experience is the mysterious. It is the source of all true art and science. He to whom the emotion is a stranger, who can no longer pause to wonder and stand wrapped in awe, is as good as dead; his eyes are closed. The insight into the mystery of life, coupled though it be with fear, has also given rise to religion. To know what is impenetrable to us really exists, manifesting itself as the highest wisdom and the most radiant beauty, which our dull faculties can comprehend only in their most primitive forms — this knowledge, this feeling is at the center of true religiousness.
>
> — A. Einstein

• By 1925 Slipher had clocked the velocities of 42 galaxies.

• Hubble's law, discovered around 1930, disclosed: *the farther away a galaxy is located, the faster it is moving.*

• Milton Humason (1891-1972) discovered distant galaxies traveling at the speed of 100 million miles an hour. During his career, he measured the speeds of 620 galaxies.

• The speed of a galaxy 70 million light years from our Sun is 3 million miles an hour. A galaxy over 1 billion light years away is traveling 126 million miles an hour. Galaxies 3 billion light years away are traveling more than 200 million miles an hour.

• Allan Sandage (1926-) compiled information on 42 galaxies ranging out in Space as far as 6 billion light years away.

• In 1960, the farthest galaxy was discovered at a distance of about 5 billion light-years. In 1976, galaxies were found 8 billion light-years away. In 1982, 4 massive galaxies were identified about 10 billion light-years away from the Earth; each galaxy, filled with at least a thousand billion stars, is traveling outward in the Universe at more than half the speed of light.

• Galaxies are known to contain single stars, solar systems, comets, double stars, star clusters, tenuous clouds of atomic hydrogen, dense clouds (containing hydrogen, oxygen, carbon and other elements), dust, planetary nebulae (glowing gases shed by maturing stars), remnants of supernovae, gas shells, wisps, filaments, neutron stars, and pulsars.

• Quasars, discovered in 1960, are believed to represent the nuclei of young galaxies. By 1982, 1,600 Quasars were discovered. Quasars, or quasi-stellar objects, are as bright as thousands of galaxies yet apparently require no more space than a single star.

• A *rich cluster* of galaxies contains hundreds of galaxies; a *great cluster*, thousands of galaxies.

• The Coma cluster of galaxies contains 11,000 galaxies; each galaxy has billions of stars.

• *Normal* galaxies are conservative in their energy use. *Active* galaxies radiate energy in a seemingly reckless way.

• Large galaxies sometimes appear to swallow small galaxies.

• Galaxies may collide.

• Some galaxies explode.

• Many galaxies seem to do a graceful dance, exchanging millions of stars with other galaxies.

• One-half of the galaxies identified by the telescopes of man are *Spiral*. The Milky Way is a Spiral galaxy. Spiral galaxies contain great quantities of dust, gas, and new, young stars.

• About one-fourth of the prominent galaxies are *Ellipticals*. Elliptical galaxies are believed to be the most numerous in the Universe. Elliptical galaxies seem to be depleted of dust and gas, and are composed almost entirely of old stars.

• *Lenticular* galaxies are very similar to spirals in form, but they lack spiral arms. These galaxies combine some of the qualities of both spirals and ellipticals.

• Other kinds of galaxies are *Irregular Galaxies, Ring Galaxies, Seyfert Galaxies, N-Galaxies,* and *Radio Galaxies*.

• Irregular galaxies have peculiar shapes; some have distorted halos, strange dust lanes, and tails and plumes in seemingly non-interacting galaxies. Only a few percent of the major galaxies are irregular.

• Most dwarf galaxies are irregulars and ellipticals. Often, they are ranged around larger galaxies.

• Some astronomers are beginning to perceive an evolutionary pattern for the galaxies. They believe that irregular galaxies are evolving into spiral galaxies, and that spiral galaxies are evolving into elliptical galaxies. They base their reasoning on the fact that young stars are located in the outer arm or arm areas of the spiral galaxies, and many old stars are in the elliptical galaxies.

• The tracing of the spiral arms of the Milky Way Galaxy began in the early 1950's. The Sun is a member of the Orion arm. The Perseus arm is farther from the center of the Galaxy. The Sagittarius arm is closer to the center of the Galaxy. Later, the Carina arm was added to the spiral structure of the Milky Way. The spiral arms are regions of star formation.

• A *satellite galaxy*, containing several billion stars, is held captive by the gravitational attraction of a larger galaxy. This may be likened to the Moon being held captive by the Earth. The Milky Way Galaxy has two satellite Galaxies revolving around it: the Magellanic Cloud, with about 20 billion stars; and the Small Magellanic Cloud, with about 2 billion stars. Scattered stars and gases connect the two Cloud satellites with each other and with the Milky Way.

• The Milky Way Galaxy, the Great Galaxy of Andromeda and about 18 other galaxies make up the cluster of galaxies called the *Local Group*. All of the Galaxies in the Local Group are moving together around a common *center* which is between the Andromeda Galaxy and the Milky Way.

THE UNIVERSE:
  Countless Galaxies of varying shapes and sizes.

SUPERCLUSTER GALAXIES:
  Varying sizes of Superclusters.
  A Supercluster may contain hundreds of billions of
    Stars or several trillion Stars.

Local Supercluster:
  Numerous clusters of
  Galaxies. The Local
  Group is located on the
  outskirts of the Local
  Supercluster.

Local Group of Galaxies:
  A Cluster of Twenty
  Galaxies, including the
  Milky Way and An-
  dromeda Galaxies.

The Milky Way:
  A Spiral Galaxy. The
  Sun is located near the
  Orion Arm of the
  Galaxy. Present estimates
  of Stars in the Milky Way
  Galaxy range from 400
  billion to 2 trillion.

Neighboring Stars:
  Stars in proximity to the
  Sun.

The Solar System:
  The Sun: A Yellow
  Dwarf Star. Nine Planets
  and their Moons,
  Asteroids and Comets.

O

Man on Earth:
  The Human Spirit.

THE UNIVERSE AND MAN

- The Andromeda Galaxy is moving relative to the Earth at a speed of 700,000 miles per hour. The Andromeda Galaxy and the Milky Way Galaxy are two spiral galaxies that spiral in opposite directions.

- The entire Milky Way Galaxy rotates at a speed of about 170 miles per second. A single rotation takes 250–280 million years.

- Beyond the Local Group of Galaxies is an area called the *Realm of Galaxies*. This Realm of Galaxies contains clusters of thousands of galaxies. Most of these galaxy clusters, along with the Local Group, are part of a supergalaxy. All of these move around a common center. Other supergalaxies in space move with other supergalaxy clusters, rotating around a common center.

- The Milky Way Galaxy is traveling 1.3 million miles per hour.

- In the early 1980's, a few astronomers theorized that the Milky Way Galaxy consists of two trillion stars, rather than the previous estimates ranging from 100 billion to 400 billion stars.

- Elements of the Milky Way Galaxy consist of approximately 73% hydrogen, 25% helium, 1% carbon, oxygen, nitrogen, neon, and 1% all others.

- There are three regions known within the innermost thousand light-years of the Milky Way Galaxy. First, there is a large zone of thin, hot, ionized gas. Within this, there is a whirlpool of dense, warm matter—and at the center, a small but very powerful energy.

- The Milky Way is noticeably brighter in Sagittarius, the direction of the galactic center.

• The Sun requires approximately 250 million years to make a complete cycle about the Galaxy.

• A massive star ends its life-cycle with a mighty supernova explosion which sends its elements back into interstellar space, where it joins material ejected by other stars.

• Only six supernova explosions have been observed in the Milky Way Galaxy in the last thousand years. The supernova of 1054 in the Constellation of Taurus was observed and recorded by the Chinese and the American Indians. Other supernova explosions in the Milky Way are known to have occurred in 1006, 1181, 1572, 1604, and 1677.

• Over four-hundred supernova explosions have been observed in other galaxies. Ten to twenty are being discovered each year in distant galaxies.

• 50–70% of all stars are members of binary star systems — two stars revolving around each other.

• The largest stars are thousands of times larger than the Sun. The smallest stars are the size of the planet Earth.

> The sun, the stars and seasons as they pass — some
> can gaze upon these with no strain of fear.
> —Horace

> Heaven's net casts wide.
>   Though its meshes are coarse,
>   nothing slips through.
> — Lao Tzu

SYMBOLS AND THE COSMOS

Geometry existed before the Creation, is co-eternal with the mind of God, *is God himself* (what exists in God that is not God himself?); geometry provided God with a model for the creation and was implanted into man together with God's own likeness—and not merely conveyed to his mind through the eyes.

—Johannes Kepler, 1616

In a circle the beginning and the end are always the same.

—Heraclitus, 500 B.C.

God loves puzzles, riddles and paradoxes. He hides clues, keys and codes in likely and unlikely places—and waits patiently for His children on Earth to discover them. Each clue to the secrets and mysteries of the Cosmos is repeated throughout the Earth in many visible forms, signs and geometrical symbols. As each clue is discovered and utilized by the human spirit, life progresses on Earth; this progression leads man starward and galaxyward.

The Creator forms a spiral-shaped shell, and waits for mankind to discover the secrets of the Spiral. God creates circular stars, planets and moons as clues to the mysteries of the Circle. The Circle, the Spiral and other links in the chain of Universal knowledge lead the minds of men to the wonders of Space.

In recent decades, astronomers have discovered that there are Galaxies of different shapes and sizes, including Elliptical Galaxies, Spiral Galaxies, Irregular Galaxies and Ring Galaxies. Mankind finds itself in a Solar System located near an arm of a Spiral Galaxy. The Milky Way has three major arms of stars: the Sagittarius Arm, closest to the galactic core; the central or Orion Arm; and the outer or Perseus Arm. The Solar System in which Man dwells is located near the Orion Arm. The Carina Arm extends from the Orion Arm.

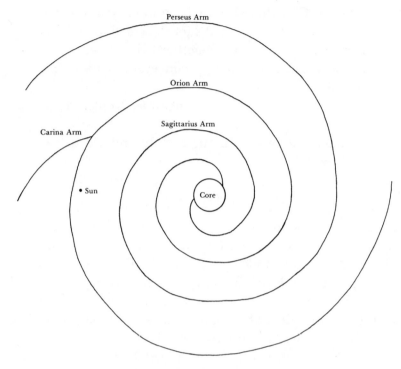

MILKY WAY GALAXY

The Spiral is a most significant Universal symbol. The word *Spiritual* is a combination of the words *spiral* and *ritual*. The many spirals found within Nature on the planet Earth contain clues to the creation of the Cosmos. The evolution of the human spirit occurs as a spiraling ascent toward Truth, Knowledge and Wisdom.

The Circle is another geometrical symbol observable throughout the Universe. The shape of each star in the Universe is circular. All planets known to man are circular. Numerous Galaxies are also circular in shape.

The knowledge of the Spiral and the Circle provides a perfect link between the mind of man and the Mind of God. The Spiral Galaxy, a spiral-shaped sea shell, the spiraling action of water, the spiraling Path of Virtue up the Mountain of Illumination — all are united by the same principle of pure truth: The Spiral.

The presence of the Spiral in the starry heavens and on the planet Earth gives to mankind an important key to comprehending the paramount symbols within a Cosmos Code. This hieroglyphic-like Code is a language known and utilized throughout the Universe. To contemplate the Spiral as part of a Cosmos Language is to prepare oneself for the Gift of Understanding.

The Spiral, the Circle and other geometrical symbols uniting the Earth with the Stars and the Galaxies are filled with the Intelligence of God. The Intelligence of God is *Holy*; therefore, each symbol present in the Universe is Holy.

To see a geometrical symbol only as a physical symbol is to miss the meaning of the spiritual power within the symbol. Nature and God have many secrets to reveal through each geometrical symbol present on Earth and in the starry heavens.

A symbol is a dimensional truth with infinite depths of meaning. To discover and experience certain dimensional depths of a key symbol is to comprehend an important clue to the Code of Cosmos. God alone determines how, when, and to whom a symbol reveals its dimensional splendor and glory.

The sages of old looked at the Cosmos through the telescope of meditation and love. Reverence for the panorama of the heavens makes of the mind a receptive and fertile energy-field in which simple Earth-truths are magnified until they reveal their Cosmos origins and purposes.

Concepts without factual content are empty;
sense-data without concepts are blind. By their
union only can knowledge be produced.
                                    —Immanuel Kant

Numerous truths are discernible by the senses of man; microscopes and telescopes, as extensions of man's senses, are able to identify these truths. Certain other truths are discovered through intuition or logic before they may be proven through the senses or instruments. Thus, Truth is twofold in that it may be discovered through instruments or through ideas.

Ideas enable man to transcend the barriers and limitations of a small planet. Ideas inspired by the soul and the spirit occur in perfect timing to the evolutionary needs of human-kind. The progression of the Universe as an orderly and mathematically-perfect creation assures man's receiving of ideas in a perfect continuity—for order and continuity are the nature of the Ongoing Spirit of God creating the Universe.

Sages, prophets and other enlightened personages versed in the sacred arts of meditation, prayer and contemplation receive timely ideas, insights and realizations regarding the key symbols being utilized by God in His creation of the Stars and Galaxies. Hence, in one moment of clear-seeing the mind may become as a powerful telescope that enables one to perceive a symbol, such as a spiral or circle, as a Cosmos Reality. In this, God has revealed a Living Truth. As these truths increase in one's heart and mind, he becomes com-municable to the Wisdom of God omnipresent throughout the Universe. Thereafter, a closeness occurs between one's heart and the Heart of God. This love-union becomes the means through which Cosmos and Earth are united in one's thinking and feeling.

The Earth is swimming in a vast sea of Energy-Radiations

of Stars and Galaxies. This Cosmos Sea is the Earth's Home; it is a Sea with mighty tides moving upon all persons at all times. The tides of the Cosmos Sea reveal their clues through the *Cycles* known to men on Earth.

The Seasonal Cycles contain great keys to comprehending four major Energy-Tides each year: Winter, Spring, Summer and Autumn. Man is being shaped and formed by these four Energy-Tides and other Creation-Cycles within the Cosmos Sea; he cannot escape the perpetual pounding of the Waves of the Cosmos Energy-Sea. These cyclic Waves are God's Will creating man in His Image and Likeness.

Men on Earth face a future in which the energy-language of the Stars and Galaxies will be recognized and understood as a vocabulary of symbols and cycles. Reverence and love toward human life and the life of Stars will invite the Blessings of God as continuous guidance, instruction and enlightenment.

A man is a dry well until God puts His Spirit upon him. The Spirit of God manifests as beautiful, compassionate and logical ideas, inspirations, insights, innovations, realizations, prophecies, revelations and creations. With the Spirit of God upon him, man becomes an unceasing Fountain of Truth flowing forth from the Eternal Wellspring of God's Love and Grace.

How could anyone observe the mighty order with which our God governs the universe without feeling himself inclined . . . to the practice of all virtues, and to the beholding of the Creator Himself, the source of all goodness, in all things and before all things?

—Nicolaus Copernicus, 1543

Philosophy is written in that vast book which stands
forever open before our eyes. I mean the universe.
— Galileo Galilei, 1564–1642

Then sawest thou that this fair Universe, were it in
the meanest province thereof, is in very deed the
star-domed City of God: that through every star,
through every grass-blade, and most through every
Living Soul, the glory of a present God still beams.
— Thomas Carlyle, 1836

SWEET INFLUENCES

Canst thou bind the sweet influences of Pleiades?
—Job 38:31

The Intelligence of God creating Constellations such as the
Pleiades sends forth their "sweet influences" upon the human
spirit. The future of man is dependent upon his working with
the Intelligence of God blessing the planet Earth through the
benefic energies of the various Constellations. Union with the
ever-present light of God's Intelligence creating the Constellations inspires one to reverently observe the Creator's Hand
forming and shaping all Stars and Galaxies, all souls and living things.

Mankind beholds the wonders of Space in three manners:
(1) atheistic, (2) agnostic, or (3) religious-spiritual. Among
those who believe in a Living God are the faithful who ac-
tively worship Him each day; other believers are not devoted
to periods of daily worship.

Worshippers differ in their attitudes toward God as the Architect of the Universe. One type of worshipper believes that
the Sun, Moon, Planets, Stars and Galaxies influence life on
Earth and are contributing to the creation of man. Another

type of worshipper does not believe that the celestial bodies have any influence on the creation of man.

The astronomer and mathematician Johannes Kepler (1571–1630), believed that the Moon caused the high tides of the ocean. Galileo, also a noted astronomer of the time, disagreed with Kepler. So it stands today: there are Truth-seekers who believe that the Moon and other celestial bodies exert an influence upon the planet Earth, and there are those who cannot accept this belief.

The Universe is *Pure Intelligence*. Every atom in the Cosmos is fulfilling an intelligent function. Each Star and Galaxy is contributing in some great and grand way to the evolving intelligence of man on the planet Earth. Alert individuals are seeking to find logical connections between the Cosmos and the intelligence of man, his soul and his being.

Every person *sees* the Universe through the telescopic lens of his consciousness. The lens of the consciousness may be covered with the soot of many prejudices and sins; or it may be a clear and clean field, perceiving the Truth accurately. The integrity and moral conscience of the individual determine what he beholds when he turns his gaze toward the starry heavens.

The atheist and the agnostic may become perfect scientists; however, their discoveries are limited to physical facts about the Cosmos. Scientists with reverent hearts and minds cast the nets of their faith into the sea of the Universe and discover sacred wisdom as well as empirical data.

Presently, many scientists are dedicated to learning about atoms and molecules. Scientists of the soul and the spirit are dedicated to learning about virtues and ethics.

The more one learns about virtues and ethics, the more he learns about God as Pure Spirit, Pure Intelligence. Virtues and ethics, being of God's Omnipresent Intelligence, are a common denominator throughout the Universe. The atoms in a carbon molecule in a distant star or on the planet Earth follow the same law of Nature; virtues and ethics also fulfill a basic law of the Universe — a law existing in every Star and Galaxy.

Scientists now know that Stars vary in their amounts of the basic elements. Some stars may be rich in certain elements; other stars may contain less of the same elements and more of other elements. These fascinating differentiations testify to a great plan of diversity established upon the identical, basic building blocks of Creation. The same principle holds true regarding the presence of virtues and ethics as component energies within the Cosmos.

The unifying "element" present in all Solar Systems is *Love*. Love is the key to comprehending the correlation between atoms and molecules, virtues and ethics. The key of love unlocks the door to the secrets and mysteries of the human heart, mind and soul; love also unlocks the door to the wonders and glories of the Cosmos.

Every Star is a creation of love. Every Galaxy is a creation of love. Man is a creation of love. When one loves, he unites with the Love of God creating all Stars, Galaxies and Man.

The Love within virtues and ethics prepares one's heart and mind for realizations and revelations about the Universe with its Time-relativities and Space-dimensionalities. God as Love is free to reveal unifying Cosmos Truths to the virtuous, the ethical, the righteous.

Through an increasing love for God and His Beautiful Intelligence creating the human spirit and the Holy Universe, one grows in Grace and Truth. The degree of one's love determines his spiritual stature, understanding and enlightenment. He who has the key of love walks the Earth as an illumined Seer, a Sage, an Apostle of the Lord of Love.

> *God is love.*
> *—1 John 4:8*

FRIENDS IN THE SKY

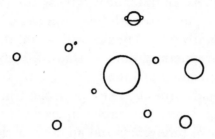

The Moon and the Planets are friends in the sky. As friends, they are constantly telling one the truth and assisting him to find happiness, peace and joy. These constant and loyal friends in the sky work with God's Will to bless, heal and anoint; they protect, enlighten and teach. To receive their friendship is to receive God's Blessings through their ordained cycles and sacred energies.

The Sun and the Stars also are friends in the sky. Each Star has a story to tell of light, truth, virtue and love. To embrace each Star as a friend is to receive the warming embrace of the Star. To embrace each Planet and the Moon as friends is to be blessed by their friendship in unique and miraculous ways.

Our friends in the sky never judge us; they live only to teach of God and His Universe. The Spirit of God fills each of His Cosmos creations. To look upon each celestial body as a friend is to see and know God as a Friend, Jesus as a friend, and the Constellation Hierarchy-Host as friends.

Jesus, the World Teacher, teaches mankind through the Solar-System cycles and energy-dynamics. To be taught by Jesus is to gain increasing understanding of the sacred purposes of each Planet, the Moon, the Sun, the Stars and the Galaxies.

All Stars and Galaxies work in friendly harmony united by love for God, their Creator. Man, in learning the principles of friendship on Earth, will gradually extend his friendship to the Moon, as his closest celestial friend; then the Sun; and then the Planets. In time, he will recognize the Stars as close friends waiting to share with him treasures of knowledge and truth. Gradually, the Galaxies will reveal their divine purposes and prophetic promises, sharing with man the true origin and meaning of Life.

To be friends with all creations in the Universe begins by applying moral and ethical principles toward life on Earth. Love, kindness, forgiveness and all other Scriptural precepts and directives are preparing man to understand the importance of friendship on Global and Cosmos levels. Those who succeed will be the new-era avatars and prophets at one with the Spirit of God creating each celestial body in the vast and mighty Universe.

THE SCIENTIFIC AND THE SPIRITUAL

> Any man who believes in God must realize that no scientific fact, as long as it is true, can contradict God. Otherwise, it would not be true. Therefore, any man who is afraid of science does not possess a strong faith.
> — Lecomte du Noüy

> Science without religion is lame,
> religion without science is blind.
> — Albert Einstein

The Truth, to be fully comprehended, must be approached from two directions: the scientific and the spiritual. The truth about a Star or a Galaxy has much to reveal in strictly scientific terms; however, there are also spiritual reasons for the existence of each Star and Galaxy.

Mankind faces a future in which scientists will become more spiritually-minded, and spiritually-minded individuals will become more scientific. In the blending of the scientific and the spiritual, man will be ennobled through a morality and rationality blessed with reason, logic and love.

In future centuries, a marriage will occur between Pure Science and Pure Religion—a marriage based upon a mutual love for the Truth as the Sovereign Principle of the Universe. Gradually, obstacles hindering the marriage between science and religion will be overcome. As in all good marriages, each will learn from the other; each will contribute to the joy of the other; and their love will result in the birth of a new and wondrous Age. The marriage between Pure Science and Pure Religion will produce the Illumination of the world.

Prejudice is one of the greatest obstacles to mankind's progress in science and in religion. Prejudice is a dark veil covering many clues to Cosmos. As the veil of prejudice is lifted, the dazzling beauty of luminous truths is discovered—truths about the Identity of Man and clues about the scientific-spiritual nature of the Universe.

In recent centuries, the birth of Pure Science was seriously threatened by religious leaders who expressed bigotry, narrow-mindedness and fear. Religious persecution of scientific genius was commonplace, and led to the creation of a chasm of separation. This temporary breach was necessary in order for Pure Science to retain its integrity and to remain a trusted voice of the Truth.

The prejudice of the priests who refused to look through Galileo's telescope is the same prejudice being expressed in modern times by scientists who refuse to look through the telescope of spirituality. The overcoming of all expressions of prejudice is essential before the human spirit can progress toward the higher levels of knowledge. Scientists prejudiced toward religiosity and religionists prejudiced toward scientists limit their comprehension of life and the Universe.

The persecution of Galileo and other scientists revealed a

blind-side in the consciousness minds of certain religious leaders. A scientist who is prejudiced toward Jesus, Buddha, Moses or any other enlightened Teacher also has a blind-side in his consciousness mind. As the prejudices of science and religion are healed, mankind will progress toward the knowledge of great truths planted as seeds of Cosmos Wisdom by men of scientific genius and by men of spiritual love.

A scientist who disregards the genius of Jesus is as remiss as a religionist who disregards the genius of Einstein. The wisdom of Einstein began a new era of knowledge regarding energy and light, Time and Space. The wisdom of Jesus opened the door to knowledge of the Dimensional Kingdoms of Righteousness and Holiness between man and God.

The *light* spoken of by Jesus and Einstein stems from the same Source of Truth. Einstein revealed a scientific comprehension of the properties and capabilities of physical light as a presence throughout the Cosmos. Jesus revealed the way of communion with the Intelligence of God within the spiritual dimensions of light.

The ethics and morals emphasized by Jesus, the Saints and other noble personages are mankind's way of creating a world-wide atmosphere of peace, harmony and good-will. The absence of ethics and morals in individuals and in nations produces misery, pain and suffering.

In recent years, scientific technology has introduced awesome weapons for destructive wars, and has diminished the health and welfare of nations through the contamination of food, water and atmosphere. Pure spiritual values are seeking to retain their integrity while certain areas of science introduce new dangers to the ethical and moral nature of man.

The new era at hand is an era in which the wisdom of prophetic scientists and spiritual sages will merge and blend until man becomes a Moral Giant as well as a Cosmos Seer. Morality on a Cosmos level assures man of his place in the Universe as a being of broad and deep intelligence. His utilization of light, love and devotion as scientific-spiritual instruments will enable him to relate to the Universe as a Holy Creation of God.

Certain dimensions of knowledge and truth open to the heart and mind only through devotion to God. Devotion expressed through daily worship is the sole means of unlocking these treasure chests of understanding.

The world of the neutrino and the quark is but a short step into the etheric zones of the inner kingdoms or dimensions of the soul and the Spirit. However, the *instruments* necessary for union with these invisible realms of Truth are *Conscience, Integrity, Morality* and *Reverence*. These beautiful expressions of the heart and mind are mankind's keys to unceasing knowledge of the Holy Universe, the Image of God, and the Mighty Laws governing Eternal Creation.

> The essence of religion is morality.
> — M. Gandhi

> Only morality in our actions can give beauty and dignity to life.
> — A. Einstein

A Comprehensive View of the Heavens

> Astronomy compels the soul to look upwards and leads us from this world to another.
> — Plato

During recent centuries, astronomy has contributed profound discoveries and prolific data regarding the starry heavens. Astronomy, as a disciplined, technological science, holds exciting prospects for the future.

Professional and amateur astronomers are directing thousands of telescopes toward the heavens. Each evening eager eyes behold the wonders of Space through powerful instruments. Through the dedicated efforts of learned astronomers, a new identity is coming to birth for mankind. This new identity is one of daring, brilliance and broadness.

In recent decades, astronomy has emerged as a pure science. In olden times, individuals who studied the Solar System and the Constellations practiced a philosophy embracing both astronomy and astrology. In ancient China, India, Egypt, South America and other lands, these astronomer-astrologers were revered for their knowledge. Kings and other leaders sought and followed their counsel.

Presently, astronomy is a factual science employing the use of sophisticated instrumentation; astrology continues to link celestial mathematics with the human condition. The mass of astrological knowledge, accumulating for thousands of years, has evolved through trial and error.

The Wise Men who followed the Star to find the Christ Child epitomize individuals of any age and time whose wisdom is derived from their knowledge of astronomy and astrology. *"Now when Jesus was born in Bethlehem of Judea in the days of Herod the king, behold, there came wise men from the east to Jerusalem, Saying, Where is he that is born King of the Jews? for we have seen his star in the east, and are come to worship him. When they had heard the king, they departed; and, lo, the star, which they saw in the east, went before them, till it came and stood over where the young child was. When they saw the star, they rejoiced with exceeding great joy."* (St. Matthew 2:1,2,9,10)

In all fields of learning, there are ethical and unethical persons. Unethical astrologers exploit their knowledge for the sake of money or fame. Ethical astrologers seek to preserve ages-old astrological truths that have survived the test of time.

A totally technological science without love lacks important qualities of the *Soul.* Where Soul is absent, Conscience and Morality are also absent. An astronomer may be a brilliant scientist; however, if he has little or no moral conscience, he cannot comprehend a Universe where Morality and Conscience play important roles. An unethical astrologer cannot understand a God of Ethics and Principles. Astronomy and astrology make their greatest contributions through hearts and minds dedicated to Truth, Ethics and a Soul-Wisdom based upon Morality and Conscience.

An astronomer or an astrologer may be an atheist, an agnostic, or a person of faith. *How* one looks at the Cosmos is determined by his attitudes, beliefs and motives.

A minister or priest who feels no enthusiastic love for the Stars and expresses no desire to learn of the Moon, the Sun and the Planets cannot inspire the members of his flock to expand their concepts of the Creator. A strong and deep love for God as Pure Truth compels one to learn of His beautiful Universe and to share this priceless knowledge with others.

Over the ages, seers, prophets, gurus and other holy personages have explored the heavens through their hearts' love for God—a love expressed through worship and devotion. The heart's love, when conjoined with a mind dedicated to Pure Truth, makes a worshipper receptive to inspired thoughts during and after reverent prayer, meditation and fasting. These thoughts and realizations are then inherited by future generations. It was through such thoughts that spiritual giants of the past left to the world a heritage of Scriptural wisdom and knowledge.

A comprehensive view of the heavens can be attained only by blending the wisdom of the past with the knowledge gained by modern-day science. This blending requires that one study Astronomy, Ethical Astrology, Scriptural Wisdom, and Symbolic Myths.

For countless ages, the human spirit has sought to comprehend the meaning of life, being and existence. The modern-day era provides unique opportunities to unite past and present, and thereby gain a clear perception of the future. The keys to understanding mankind's past and future may be found in the Stars and Galaxies. The ancients planted the seeds; the present-day prophets in various scientific, philosophical and spiritual disciplines are watering the seeds; and the future wise men will reap the golden harvest of Absolute and Universal Truth.

A comprehensive view of the heavens as a physical and spiritual creation occurs through a *synthesis* of the scientific, the mystical-intuitional, and the sacred gift of revelation. When the soul, heart and mind are equally involved in the search for Cosmos Truth, the Spirit of God provides the intuition and the revelation.

Infinity and Eternality, Timelessness and Spacelessness cannot be understood by the intellect alone; the soul and heart must also be utilized as instruments of understanding. The heart and mind are easily diverted from the Path of Pure Truth by the temptations and pleasures of the physical world; however, the soul remains eternally centered in Pure Truth. All who truly seek to learn of God's Universe and to contribute to its Creation work to become pure in body, heart, mind and soul, that the Spirit of God may reveal to them the splendors and glories of Pure Truth and Eternal Love.

> *Blessed are the pure in heart: for they shall see God.*
>
> —*St. Matthew* 5:8

MOVEMENT AND THE MUSIC OF GOD

> The music of God has sent forth His universe, His galaxies, His stars.
>
> —Ann Ree Colton

> Music is the only spiritual entrance to a higher world of knowledge.
>
> —Beethoven

The aim and final reason of all music should be
nothing else but the glory of God and the refresh-
ment of the spirit.

—Bach

To sum up the nature of this scientific revolution
in a single phrase, we are finding that the universe
is composed not of matter but of music.

—Dr. Donald Hatch Andrews

Praise ye the Lord. Praise God in his sanctuary:
praise him in the firmament of his power. Praise
him for his mighty acts: praise him according to his
excellent greatness. Praise him with the sound of
the trumpet: praise him with the psaltery and harp.
Praise him with the timbrel and dance.

—Psalm 150:1-4

His form is everywhere, all pervading . . .
Everywhere is Shiva's gracious dance made
manifest . . .
He dances with Water, Fire, Wind and Ether.
Thus our Lord dances ever in the court.

—Hindu Scripture

With the creation of the universe the dance too
came into being, which signifies the union of the
elements. The round dance of the stars, the constellation of planets in relation to the fixed stars, the
beautiful order and harmony in all its movements,
is a mirror of the original dance at the time of
creation.

—Lucian
2nd Century Roman poet

And just as he who dances with his body, rushing
through the rotating movements of the limbs, acquires a right to share in the round dance, in the
same way he who dances the spiritual dance, always
moving in the ecstasy of faith, acquires a right to
dance in the ring of all creation.
—St. Ambrose
Bishop of Milan, 4th Century

There is a music of the minutes, a symphony of the
seconds, a dance of the days.

There is a melody of the months, a seranade of the seasons,
a rhythm of the years.

There is a crescendo of the decades, a rhapsody of the centuries, a glory of the ages.

God creates through music and movement. Wherever
energy and movement are present in God's Holy Universe,
there is music.

*When the morning stars sang together, and all the sons
of God shouted for joy . . ."* *(Job 38:7)* The Stars sing in a
Cosmos chorus of light-energy tones. The Galaxies are as
sound chambers throughout the Universe. Each Galaxy is in
concert with the other Galaxies in its cluster. All Galaxy
Clusters fulfill their unique soundings and sendings.

Man is learning to move and sing and dance in perfect accord with the Cosmos Creation of Stars and Galaxies. He
begins by opening his ears to the Voice of God; his heart, to
the Love of God. The Universal Music then lifts him up and
moves him along on the song-currents of the Stars and the
sound-currents of the Galaxies. His days come into order, for
he is one with the Divine Order. His life comes into joy-
harmonies, for he has become part of the joy-harmonies of
God's Love-Universe.

In the world of man, there is music within every kind of

physical, emotional, mental and spiritual movement. The thoughts moving through one's mind; the emotions being expressed inwardly and outwardly; the physical body's activities; the soul in its energy-releasements—all are part of the music of Universal Creation.

As the beauty, order and harmony of God's Cosmos Music move into one's heart, mind and being, his emotions, thoughts and life become a unified expression of beauty, order and harmony at one with the whole of Creation. Individuals in flowing harmony with the greater musics of God within the Cosmos are in perfect timing with life-processes and soul-grace harmonies; they are in timing with the Coinciding Principle and other mighty Principles. These inspired personages serve God and their fellow man with Effortless Effort, for they are centered within the Providential Grace and Love of God.

SOUL DANCE

The Dance of the Soul is an Energy Dance.
The Dance of the Soul is in rhythm to the Music of God's Love.
The Music of God's Love is in His Laws governing and creating the Universe.
The Dance of the Soul is a Joyful Dance—for the Universe is being created through the Creator's Joy.
When one creates in the Name of God, he enters into the Creator's Joy, and therefore he is doing the Soul Dance.

The Energies of the Soul are Divine Energies.
These Energies, being Divine, are Dimensional— uniting one with the Dimensional Kingdoms of God.

*The Dimensional Kingdoms of God are Grace-
     Kingdoms lighted by the Love of God's Eternal
     Spirit.
All who love are Soul Dancers doing their Joyful
     Dance, inspired by the Music of Cosmos
     Creation.*

*The Word of God is the Purest of all Energies, All
     Tones, all Lights. To hear the Word of God is
     to be lifted up by the Invisible Currents of
     Grace.
The Currents of Grace move one back and forth,
     in and out, up and down, in harmonious
     rhythms of Love-Joy and Love-Ecstasy. This is
     the Soul's Dance—the Dance of Eternal Life, the
     Dance from Star to Star in sublime and
     ascending heights.*

GALAXY M-51. *Courtesy of Mark Sobel*

3

THE MORALITY UNIVERSE

*There is no greater system of Morality than
the system of the Universe. It is a Morality
Universe.*

THE VITA PRINCIPLE

The Ten Commandments are the music of Virtue.

The Archetypal Atma or the *Word* is the Central and First
Atom holding together all Galaxies, all Suns, all Earth-
systems, all Creations. The Archetypal Atma is the Godhead
from which all Energy and Vibration stem as Intelligible
Consciousness.

The Archetypal Intelligible is *God*. God as Soul and Spirit
is Godhead in man. By rates and measures, men record the
rotation and movement of worlds within worlds, whereby the
Intelligible makes known His Manifestation as Consciousness
in Man.

There cannot be one thing between the Stars, the Planets
and man which can go backward in Universal movement. In
the Law of Creation, man must move forward with and
within the Creation of God. In this, he is blessed; if he thinks
he can reverse the Law of Creation, he is laggard, tamas.

The Universe is a great system of Morality. It functions as
a totality system of Morality whereby God uses His Spirit of
Creation as a Constant. This Constant stimulates Morality
and Virtue.

All eternity systems exist in Intelligible states of perfecting,
that they may be perfected as channels for the Spirit of God.
All eternity systems communicate and are mediators for
Universal Spirit. Eternity systems are yoked to God and never
absent from the state of Creating for God.

God seeks to see at all times the fulfillment of the harmonic
blending between all forms of life — conscious, sentient and
sub-sentient. Every particle of energy upholding the life-
systems is intelligence awaiting to become awareness as a constant state in consciousness.

Mediation between eternity systems is gained through a
continuity Intelligible flow of Spirit as consciousness. That
which is sub-sentient will become sentient. That which is sentient will become conscious.

In thought and the processes of thinking, nothing is lost in
the divine harmony of unison and mediation. The Spirit of
God is the Quickener. Each form in life is awaiting its
Quickening.

Man is in danger of breaking the chain of his specie
through corruption in habits, perversions in sex, blind
bewilderment in his psychological behaviour, and godlessness
in his apathies. God has always used His cataclysms and
catastrophies, His volcanoes, His floods and His glacier-
periods to shock men out of their Kali-Yuga states. In this
Kali-Yuga, God is using the Cosmos, that men may experience a Cosmos union with His Universe and with His Eternal Being.

The only thing man possesses which makes him a unique
individualized *soul-being* is conscience. If he seeks to succeed
in the world without conscience, he is doomed and fated to

death as to individuality. Such a death throws one back upon the wills of those less-evolved. He becomes the victim of the masses, of persons, of institutions, or of life-styles. His individual birthright having been sold through denial of conscience, he becomes a part of the mass.

Man has yet to master duality thinking, which creates in him a divided consciousness through which he sees all things as the other or the adversary. Until he masters the negativity side of his expression, he will remain split, separate, apart from God, from all others in the world.

True ritual is practiced by knowing God as the Omnipresence. When one attains this, he has command of the Vita Principle supporting Morality, Goodness, Order, Peace. He has attained Omnipresence in his own nature, whereby Omniscience is expressed as Knowing or Niscience.

To live within awareness of interrelatedness of all life moves one beyond relativity. His knowledge comes from a direct communion interflow of unlimited states of consciousness.

To take command of the Vita Principle each day and to live within this third aspect of the mind and of Knowing is to become a master of perception. Unimpressed by the gravitational pull of gross psychic energy, such persons live with equanimity in both the physical and spiritual worlds.

The Vita Principle furnishes the Ethic. When one is out of alignment with the order of equanimity upholding morality, he offends the Vita Principle. He fails to express himself ethically as a moral being with pure motive and with chaste intent.

The reservoir of the Vita Principle is expressed through man through Pisces, Aries, Taurus, Gemini and Cancer. These Constellation Stations or Houses are sustained by day-by-day works of morality in service to God.

The Vita Principle supports the Ethic of the Lord Jesus in one's soul. Through prayer, meditation and dedication, one

draws upon the Vita Principle whereby his actions are considered to be ethical. Jesus laid down the Ethic for the life of
the soul in the world of man in His Sermon on the Mount and
in His reminders of the necessity to live within the
Commandments.

Until the coming of Jesus, men expressed themselves
blindly, drawing upon the subconscious, instinctual laws.
After the coming of Jesus, man became his own maker.
Through the use of his conscience, he became mentally aware
of the need to live rightfully, lovingly. The evils of one's
wrongdoing exist as primal, instinctual remnants in the subconscious. These are moved out in initiatory periods and
cycles.

> *The Power of God in me is bringing peace,*
>   *purifying.*
> *The Presence of God in me is flowing to the*
>   *need—healing, cleansing.*
> *The law of righteousness comes forth into the*
>   *need.*
> *Let peace come. Let praise of God return.*

CONSCIENCE AND MORALITY

> *If man has a morality conscience on the*
> *level of the Universe, he will stand upright in*
> *the Christed stature.*

From the first breath of life, man in the Earth as a consciousness being is in an incessant state of Initiation stemming
from the energies of the Planets, the Sun, the Moon and the
Earth. These energies in the Earth initiate man.

Saturn and the Sun introduce one to knowledge of the

Planets. The Moon does not introduce one to knowledge of the Planets. The Moon has knowledge of the Sun; and the Moon acts as a mirror between man's knowledge of the Planets and the knowledge of himself in the Earth.

The Moon belongs to two energy forces: the Sun and the Earth. It must serve the Sun and the Earth. All persons undergo initiation under Saturn, that they may become car-bonized and eventually have Sun Initiation to become diamonds through the Sun.

Every 28 years there is something between Saturn and the Moon that creates for man a preparation for the 30-year Cycle. The 28th year approaching the 30-year Saturn Cycle triggers the quickening for these Cycles.

Saturn rules the conscience. The Capricorn Prototype under the rulership of Saturn influences the conscience of others. Jesus, as a Capricorn, used Saturn to reinforce the conscience of the earth peoples.

Man reaches Jesus through contrition, confession and ad-mission of wrongdoing, and thus frees his conscience. A stabilized conscience under Jesus is a Saturn blessing.

The whole system of the Earth is a Morality-system. The *Golden Rule* is the Essential Morality.

There are three Moralities. One is the *Eternal Morality* which is contained in: *"Thou shalt love the lord thy God with all thy heart, and with all thy soul, and with all thy strength, and with all thy mind." (St. Luke 10:27)*

There is an *Eternity Morality* for a cosmic system. This is: *"Thou shalt love thy neighbor as thyself" (St. Matthew 22:39)* and *"Do unto others as you would have them do unto you."*

The third Morality, containing these two, is destined to ex-tend the soul of man. This Morality as taught by Jesus is: *"Love ye one another."*

There is a Total Morality in the creation of the Universe.

In an eternity system, this Morality acts as the collective psyche or Composite Soul, which moves the soul of the individual ever forward toward perfection. When man is unresponsive to his individual conscience, the world-psyche or conscience reinforces the Universal Morality through the Law of God.

When man is awakened to his own conscience through Self-Realization, the total Universal Morality showers him with blessings and prospering. But until that time, the world-psyche punishes him who is devoid of realization to conscience.

Nature or Prakriti, through the Time-system, phases out what is no longer useful. Nature, as an aspect of the world-psyche, punishes the trivial and the frivolous, the malformed or the contrived. All things of untruth come under the penalty of limitation and destruction.

Nature uses the Coinciding Laws to build man, to interfuse the strengths of man. Nature also uses the Destroying Principle to limit that which is not reinforced by a true morality.

What the governor is in a car or motor vehicle, the conscience is in the moral life. The conscience is both the governor and law functioning in the soul and physical life of man. One born without a governor or conscience-functioning is defective in character. There can be no morality without conscience.

There is a sincere morality and an insincere morality. A person having insincere morality forgets his own sins and condemns others. A sincere morality looks with compassion upon others who are snared into the life of sin, for in the sincere-morality person there is the fire of remembered pain caused by willful sinning.

Undigested sinning produces a divided conscience. Releasement from sin comes from birth to virtue. Will, when healed, becomes a pure reformer and shaper.

One who has sinned carelessly has yet to face the whole blessing of a clean conscience. He who has sinned carelessly attracts to himself those who sin against him in equal measure of carelessness. And he who delights in sinning mocks God and His Divine Law.

One who says, "Look at me, I am a reformed sinner," is inviting temptation. To blow the horn of virtue is non-virtue.

A hardened sinner is like a rock, but when the virtue of the Holy Spirit is within him, he becomes a spring within the rock. From this come the crystal-clear waters, which are compassionate, healing, peace-giving.

A gray conscience produces the critical mind and also the hypocritical life and life-style. A gray conscience is neither black, totally sinful, nor white, totally pure.

A person expressing the state of gray conscience is amoral, agnostic, in his thought processes. Having difficulty in respecting himself, he seeks to transpose his conscience-conflicts through adverse criticisms of the Morality Principle in others. The field play of his conscience-structure is played out in his seeking to find fault with systems, with institutions, with persons. Being unable to relinquish the sensuality-side of his own self-indulgence, he sees in the wrongdoing of others the fault and the sin.

Such persons in a pulpit are fanatical reformers. On the domestic scene, they are uncommunicating husbands or fathers, mothers or wives. They feel that everything that goes wrong is someone else's fault or it is contributed to by an inexplicable cause. The transposing of their own sin-inferences keeps them in a constant state of electrified thought-irritation. Eventually, such persons invite into their physical lives heavy challenges affecting their pride and vanities. Also, this constant state of conscience-irritation affects the central nervous system, creating health disorders.

In the spiritual life, one must die to a laden conscience; he must mark and trace each gross, dense particle existing as blind-self.

Through gradual procedures of spiritual realization and initiation, a gray conscience becomes white. One sees then with the whole seeing of the Divine all others who are caught together in the same sea of compulsion, whereby they earn and learn and grow in states of God-Realization.

A clean conscience enables one to see the Image of God in all others and in all things. All Saints and Sages have attained the pure white stone and wear the garment of spirituality through the birth to Conscience.

There is a religious conscience, a race conscience, a family conscience, a family-atom conscience, a gene conscience, a nation conscience, an ethic-conscience, and a spiritual conscience.

Conscience and memory are twin functions of the soul. Conscience is yang; memory is yin.

Soul, entitized as consciousness, dies not. Solar systems die, as mortal man dies.

Inanimate voids are created when conscience and consciousness cease to relate to the redeeming nature of God. When evil becomes greater than the spirit of good, the Spirit of God cannot function with His Increase in an eternity system. The axis pole commanding an eternity system maintains its balance when men think God-ward rather than self-ward.

With the coming of the Christ, man began to reach toward God-Realization. The subjective inclinations in all souls in the Earth are to create with and for God. The experiment in self as ego is being translated into self as soul.

This Earth has begun to turn to God through the Christ.

Henceforth, it will maintain an inclination to immortalize the sensibilities of the Earth system, and thus live out its days and units of measure according to Galaxy-progression.

If the inhabitants of an eternity system mass together in an amorality-orgy of lawlessness, the result is similar to a car out of the right lane, upsetting the total traffic system of the lawful. An unspiritualized eternity system is a doomed system. The inanimate matter in an eternity system no longer used with reverence destroys itself. Souls inhabiting a non-cooperating system flow into other eternity systems suited for them.

Universal order has a destructive side. The Destroying Archetypes explode an eternity system which has been over-abused by inhabitants who refuse to live within the Order of God's Increase and Morality sustaining the total Universe.

Eternity systems fall into twilight states and undergo inversions of gravity when the collective consciousness in a planet defies the law of progress which can only be rightful in the Spirit of God by living within the law of love, of goodness, of peace. Thus, evil is limited in an eternity system, for the Law of God and His retributions are many and varied.

The present state of man's amorality is straining the equilibrium of this present time in this eternity system. Wars, preparation for carnage in war, and victory through war are immoral. The Spirit of God forgives, but if sin is indulged in for its pleasure within the pleasure principle, a total disorienting begins. Death becomes a reality. Pain and suffering reveal to man his need of God, his need of Law, his need of Love.

Any form of action committed with an evil heart is sin — and the consequence of this sin is suffering. Dying to an evil heart is the greatest struggle. Lust and hatred, greed and envy, pride and ambition have no place in the heart. The heart is a vessel of love, the divine cave where the Supreme Lord seeks to dwell.

Jesus passes on the Father's Forgiveness through redemption. Redemption becomes grace through which one bears his sins of the past and makes restitution in the present. Restitution in the present fortifies one against sinning in the future.

To receive redemption through the Bread passed on from the Father through Jesus and on to the one taking the Bread is to receive life, life more abundantly, which is healing.

There is but one sickness—the sickness of sin. Every sickness is a deviation from Law.

Rightful acceptance in rightful spirit assures one of rightful health, vitality. Love of life and enthusiasm for life is health as God in man.

There can be no rightful restitution without a righteous heart. A righteous heart within the rightful Spirit of God will never go astray.

> *Blessed are they which do hunger and thirst after righteousness: for they shall be filled.*
> —*St. Matthew 5:7*

APOLOGY

> *Therefore if thou bring thy gift to the altar, and there rememberest that thy brother hath ought against thee; Leave there thy gift before the altar, and go thy way; first be reconciled to thy brother, and then come and offer thy gift.*
> —*St. Matthew 5:23,24*

Confession begins when one says to those he has wronged: "Forgive me. I apologize. I have sinned against you."

A warm apology given with a right heart brings people closer together. It is a form of healing in relationships.

The self-righteous person never apologizes, feeling that it

demeans him and puts him under the will of another. This is an *out-sight* rather than an *insight* action.

There can be no true and total repentance and rectification of karma until a person—through a natural desire—moves forth to rectify all relationships.

A Lesser Self-Genesis sickness is arrogance expressed as stepping upon the feelings of others. Failing to see that one can offend in his own actions is a Lesser Self-Genesis disease.

Every true disciple of the inner and higher life should seek to temper his hyper-sensitivity by recognizing that he himself may have fault in his own nature.

It is a gracious art to apologize. It is a gracious art to apologize for one's absence from spiritual instruction.

The Four Moralities

In man's domain, there is a *mental morality* in thinking based upon the integrity of the mind; an *emotional morality* based upon the use of love; an *etheric morality* based upon obedience to Nature's laws; and a *physical morality* based upon one's acts and actions.

A person may have mental morality but not have emotional morality. Moral-judgment comes from the emotions. Learning-judgment comes from the mind.

Natural grace supports purity—this is a law. Amorality produces stress in environments and in those who practice it.

The Ethic of Jesus is that which gives man Morality. One cannot have ethic unless he has morality.

Courage for ethic and principles is one of the highest points in integrity. The Moral Principles are the supports of one's ethical, everyday life.

The Old Testament is a book of Mercy. The New Testament is a book of Forgiveness. Each of these is a Gift of God: Forgiveness and Mercy.

The basic core of the ethic is Forgiveness—and its chief functioning is Reconciliation. Forgiveness is the juice in the stalk of life.

When a person strays into adulterous acts with the opposite sex, the brace-work of morality is shaken. In adultery, the marriage sheath is damaged. However, if there is a degree of grace—and willingness on the part of the two involved in the marriage state—the sheath can be mended. After adultery, contrition and repentance and acts of purification will retrieve morality.

When a person offends the generative act through perversion, the brace-work of morality is shattered. In acts of perversion, a shattered morality opens the door to mental derangement through which the forces of the dark obsess and take possession of a deviated mind.

Duty is the first virtue in the Maya system. Duty holds together the morality of the people. When duty takes control of habit within the Will of God, one has joined the community of builders in the angelic and in the world kingdoms.

Where reverence is, God can abide. One must first have *Altar-reverence* to experience *Altar-awareness*; from this, he has Soul-Transmitting power. Then comes the Pure Logos, repeating the Archetypal Word.

PARENT AND CHILD MORALITY

> *Train up a child in the way he should go: and when he is old, he will not depart from it.*
> —*Proverbs 22:6*

Men must extend their communications within the family environments. Parents must now seek to become coordinators with the Morality of the Universe, that they may pass on to their childern the morality states of being and becoming.

Children are divided into two classes concerning their

knowing of God: one enters this world as a mystic heart and devotee; the other enters as an experimenter and a scientist-to-be. Worship must nourish and feed these two types of children.

The inquiring child is a scientist and explorer. His attention span is short. Permissive parents cannot control this child or discipline him in a worshipful environment. However, he is an observer of movement and is looking for the cause. One teaches this child about God through symbolic interpretation of God as to Cause.

The mystic-heart child or devotee enters the world with an intuitive heart. He comprehends God through feeling, faith. He has little difficulty uniting with the angelic kingdom. Being neither presumptuous nor precocious, such children can be expected, especially from the ages of two to eight, to experience many inner illuminative, revelatory insights unique, totally afresh with impressionable recollections of God as Reality and Truth.

The devotee child is more passive in the worshipful classroom. His frailty lies in passivity and lack of retention on the mental level.

>   *Honour thy father and thy mother.*
>   *—St. Matthew 19:19*

A teachable child is obedient to his parents and respectful of his parents. In the future, when he becomes a parent, he will respect the child to whom he gives birth.

Reverence works through magnetism to attract souls to each other. Respect is the doorway to reverence. Veneration is the thread holding together the Great Souls who are the parents of instruction.

A person who does not know how to honor his father and mother does not know how to honor his Teacher, for his Teacher is the parental figure in the spiritual life.

Honoring one's parent means doing honorable, creditable

and lawful things in the world. When one lives the moral life, he is doing the Will of the Father. He honors his Father in Heaven and his physical father.

An amoral physical parent has no soul-claim upon a spiritual child. If one does not pass on to his child or children a *core* of integrity and reliability, they will be unfit for themselves and for society.

Children who fear begin to lie at an early age. As they grow and develop on competitive levels of life, they learn to lie to please others. In seeking to please others, they seek to make pleasure for others, thus avoiding discipline and repentance.

The first three things vital in the life of the parent and the child are:

1. To instill into the child the pure principles of moral integrity so that the child may protect the chastity of his pure soul-impulses.

2. The second great necessity between parent and child from the cradle to maturity is to influence the child in the smaller and greater disciplines as to the necessity to work, and thereby be self-responsible.

3. The third necessity in the rearing and molding of a child is to instill into him that he is a single unit of Spirit, body and soul with an inward and outward capacity to fulfill his own unique destiny, and that he can only accomplish this by communicating with those who walk with him and share with him in the world.

Let the child be aware of the Inner Light or the Presence of God within as an *Omnipresence* never absent. Let the child also be aware of the angels who watch over his destiny. Let the child be aware of the Guiding Inner Light.

SEXUAL MORALITY

Love without morality is disenchantment.

A pure and whole observance of morality was relinquished when the Adam humanity fell into the sexual current through astral serpentine power. This was necessary in the natural order of man's progression from the Edenic state into matter or the taking on of "coats of skin." (Genesis 3:2)

The glandular system channels the will of man. In the fall into flesh, the will of man was divided. He became a duality being, receiving choice and the power to make decision. No longer able to hear the direct Voice of God, he began to rely upon himself, and thus began the trials of tribulation and joy in Earth. The only "original sin" is that man fell from Edenic grace not by wrongdoing but by a mystic veiling.

The true procreative life is a life of reverence for all sexual forms governing the necessity for birth into the world.

Sexual trials are sometimes experienced in the life of an initiate when he is being tried as to purity of attitude toward his own sexual impulse; he undergoes self-research as to prudery regarding others, as well as sexual judgment of others.

Dwelling on sex for sex is lust. Through reverent meditation and pure devotion, one lifts the kundalini's sacral procreative fire.

An ethical spiritual Teacher will not encourage or give license to indulge in or gratify sensual sexual desires. If one is married, sexual life is a responsibility and should be entered into with reverence.

In the female initiate, during menopause, the glands are sometimes overstimulated by use of hormones. If this occurs, she should hold fast to her moral principle and trust in her Angel of Pure Desiring to help her to use the sexual compulsions on a higher level of emotion and mind.

One cannot excuse immoral acts on the basis of permissiveness. Sex unsanctioned by the laws of heaven is a consuming fire burning up the vital ethers of the higher will, leaving scars and regrets upon the memory and conscience.

When one uses his procreative tides rightfully in his earlier years, he will naturally transmute the sexual force into higher spiritual impulses. Should he have failed to do this, negative sexual trials will occur in varied manners:

1. Aversion to the sexual force as a natural part of life of the world.

2. Vulgarity in thoughts of sex.

3. Prudery and frigidity as to sex.

4. Secret hidden acts of sex — as adultery, masturbation, etc.

5. Refusing to admit sex exists.

6. Judging the sex life of others, forgetting one's own sex offense.

7. Repugnance to one's own means of being physically born.

Sensual sex, as yet being so little understood, often takes possession of one's reasoning faculties. The darkened forces acting as tempters seek to divert one from the ethical use of sex. If one is caught into this diverting snare, he burns. This is why Paul said: *"It is better to marry than to burn."* (1 Corinthians 7:9)

Every man's sexual life is his own; no one can judge. Only the soul knows what one must learn. A heart of purity and a mind free of lust assure one of a contented life.

Sexual sensuality uses the sex force not thinking of the consequences as to person or persons. Sexual sensuality is the sub-brute factor in the unevolved sensual man, seeking to degrade his reverence and humanity for other men.

A race or a mass of persons using sensuality sexually is a brutal race, inflicting base acts and brutal ways upon their fellow man.

Sex, as a function of pure love, blesses; providing union of all of the biological rhythms of life; producing glandular health of the body; giving harmony to one's conscience regarding procreation and creation.

When the Male Initiate comes up before the Initiating Ones in the spiritual worlds — in his dreams and in his waking consciousness — he is tested for morality, for sexual honesty, for integrity. No labor of essential worth is given to any initiate, male or female, unless basic character and integrity have undergone evaluation by the authorized Initiators in the spiritual worlds.

There is money morality; friendship morality; sexual morality; come-and-go morality; and a *self* morality, which is soul integrity. The Christ morality is a morality of supreme values. Sooner or later, a person will shift to these values.

God gives to everyone choice — and one can be his own ruin or his own resurrection. There are those who go out of this life with a grunt, and those who go out of this life with a song of praise. Those who go out with a song of praise are those who have faced themselves.

What one refuses to learn through the mind, he learns through the grind. Every lie one has ever told, he will have to live out through reincarnation.

ABORTION

One who has failed to be accepted into a womb — or has been aborted — will remain suspended in the matrix of pre-birth until he is accepted by the souls through whom he had chosen to incarnate. It is karma's action in both worlds that the law of attraction seals the edict of karma.

A woman who aborts a child through a willful denial of birth will eventually conceive the same soul into her womb. The karma will be assessed in time according to the evolvement of souls. Thus, an imprudent and neglectful person through the precision of karmic law will attract again the same soul who has been denied. On the second round of conception, the karmic impact between such souls will be multiplied and magnified, causing untold misery between child and parents.

Every child denied the right to the womb will have to be born through the same womb that denied him. This is the Law of Karma. Any mitigation of this Law can be balanced by a rejecting mother and father only by selfless acts and assumption of burdens for the weak and the helpless.

Abortion is a violation of the womb and its creative processes. In the law of karma, it is inevitable that a child born after a willful abortion is heavily laden with karma. It also is deficient in its own immunizing processes due to the disruption of the cyclic nurturing within the 9-months period.

Any cyclic flow of Nature which begins in the primordial impulse, when interfered with, results in some abnormality.

Even though a person rejects the child, it is best to bear the child in full. The body of the woman who has subjected herself to abortion is outraged and offended for life. Certain defenses are partially and, in some cases, totally nullified.

LAW AND TRUTH

> *Thy righteousness is an everlasting righteousness,*
> *and Thy law is the truth.*
>> —*Psalm 119:142*

The Presence of God is present in His Law. The Commandments are the alphabet of a moral life, without which a spiritual life is impossible.

In some systems of psychology, there is a revolt against the Ten Commandments. The more one keeps the Ethic and the Commandments, the more he is free from tyranny. The only time one has total detachment is when he is full of Ethic and full of the Commandments.

Truth has many doors. The Greater Door to the Truth is the Law. He who goes through the Door of the Law unites with the Greater Reality supporting the Cosmos.

All things originate from one Essence. There is but one Law, one Truth. Truth and Law are one. To live in Truth is to be lawful. To live in Law is to be truthful.

Wisdom is the wife of Truth.

The more extreme the deviation from the Law, the greater the suffering. The greater the spiritual knowledge, the more intense the karma. An initiate failing to remain within the accelerated timing of his evolvement will by deviation invoke upon himself the intensities of his karma condensed in one situation painful and sorrowful.

"And Jesus said unto him, No man, having put his hand to the plough, and looking back, is fit for the kingdom of God." (St. Luke 9:62) He who puts his hand on the plow cannot look back. The greater the light, the greater the fall.

The majority of people in the world today have not begun to live in Moses' law, let alone Jesus' law. The subjective karmic law which is presently being invoked in this age, and the need for the Commandments to live by, are at hand. The world-conscience cannot be lifted by angelic or Jesus' mediation until men take hold of the Commandments so that they might move forward into the *Jesus Ethic* of love ye one another.

Fulfilling of the Law gives one the protection of Law. He who recognizes the Law, and abides in it, is a responsible person.

Karma determines that when a person has a weak sense of loyalty in a past life, he must be fixed in coming lives in a placement where *duty* is the first requirement.

Cursing begins when Law is offended. Bad fortune is a curse falling upon the meandering and the malingering soul. The Undersoul is filled with heated retaliation-reflexes of unlawful malice against the Laws of God.

Force produces sin, and humility produces glory. It is good when one is riding the waves of the Law.

Bondage to the Law is fear. Living within the Law is Love. One is in bondage to the Law when he does not serve within the Law. When one begins to serve within the Law, he is a liberator of souls; he is also free, and no longer under bondage.

One should hold fast by being steadfast. He should act through the Law and think through Love. Grace comes after having used the Law with Love.

The soul-powers can work in no other way save through the Law. Every Law observed frees the soul-powers.

The Law has a progressive selectivity. Without deviation, spiritual Law selects hearts of Truth, that it might keep the equilibrium-balances within the Word of God. Spiritual Law does not select the lawless to manifest the Law of God; but only one who has a heart, mind, soul, strength and vision on the Word of God is *chosen* to speak His Word as a living presence in the world.

> *He who beholds My Word with a fixed vision and lives My Word with a consistent heart is called to teach My Word, My Way, My Truth, My Life.*

Morality Initiation Through the Ten Commandments and the Zodiac

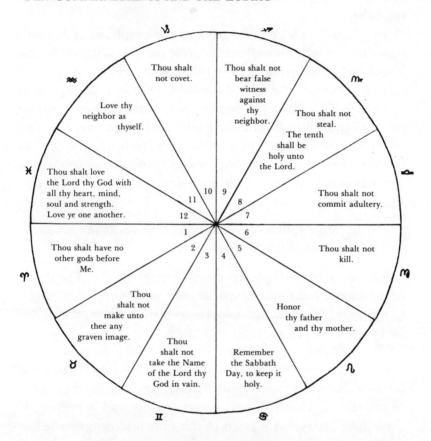

The *Commandments Zodiacal Mandala* is divided into twelve parts. These correlate to the Zodiacal Houses in the horoscope of a person. Each House contains a hidden or concealed Commandment. When all Commandments within the Houses are fulfilled, this produces a glorified or exalted horoscope. *If one meditates upon this Chart, he will receive etheric blessings through the Commandments.*

The left side of the Chart expresses the right side of the brain. The right side of the Chart expresses the left side of the brain.

To discover where one activates the emphasis of his own morality through his soul-record, one should contemplate the Ten Commandments as they relate to karma or grace.

The encasement circle of the Constellations, as expressed by man in the zodiacal circumference, is maintained in twelve states of morality. When one unites with the understanding of the Greater-Constellation influences, he opens the door to the memory of morality-knowledge through the use of the Ten Commandments, which work through the Hierarchy and Planetary Mediation.

> *When I touch, I feel. My feeling holds the clue to my motivation in desire.*

The sense of touch is expressed through desire. The desire or emotional body is a compacted-energy feeling-body. Man's morality is expressed and experienced through his emotional body or his desire nature.

The emotional body has its throne in the First House of one's chart; the etheric body, in the Fourth House; the physical body, in the Seventh House; and the mental body, in the Tenth House. The planets, ruling and aspecting in these four Houses as related to the four bodies, provide one with past-life memory as to the expression of his emotional morality, his etheric, instinctive morality, his physical-body morality and his mental morality. From these four aspects of morality, character may be gauged and weighed.

When man is fully developed in the great Cosmic Day of this eternity system, he will have processed twelve creative energies in his physical, etheric, emotional and mental bodies. In this, he will have developed a consciousness which will open him to the Galaxy-Gate knowledge of Total Cosmos.

There are seven Houses that initiate man specifically in his morality states of day-by-day conscience and consciousness: Leo, Virgo, Libra, Scorpio, Sagittarius, Capricorn and Aquarius. These are the Houses through which man forms his character and expands his mind. By observing the Commandments correlating to these seven Houses, one is initiated in everyday life.

The seven Houses of Leo through Aquarius involve one in initiatory processes related to work, works and service; personal involvement through association; and especially give him the power to overcome his material concepts of life. His most personal virtues relate to these seven Houses and the Commandments expressed therein. One has physical-earth powers through these seven Houses because he has used enterprising powers of the mind successfully in former lives.

The five remaining Commandments activated on the soul-side of one's chart correlate to the awakened and the unawakened faculties of the soul. In mastering the use of his five senses, one extends his sense-perception and unites with his soul and spiritual potential. His longing and yearning for a centered, internal peace is worked out through the five Houses representing the mature as well as the unawakened soul-powers and unmanifested soul-proclivities: Pisces, Aries, Taurus, Gemini and Cancer.

The Houses beginning with Pisces and going upward to the 10th and 9th Houses provide the perfected soul-inclinations to the Initiate of the Earth system.

Each House is an energy field bearing the record of past-life Maya experience.

FIRST HOUSE: ARIES. *Thou shalt have no other gods before Me*. Recognition of God. Thou shalt not worship the ego. The ego and its works are perishable without acknowledgment of God. The First House relates to the ego until one places God there. By the worship of God as the

One, one's ego becomes a flawless instrument for the True Self or Higher Self.

The First House in one's Zodiacal Chart expresses the desire body or the emotional body and the ego; it reveals the shell of Maya or the ego built from the past life by karma or by grace. The First House also relates to the *appearance* of the person; how he looks to others.

SECOND HOUSE: TAURUS. *Thou shalt not make unto thee any graven image.* The Second House reveals one's stewardship from past lives, whether material or spiritual. When one uses the Second House to earn in service to God, he prospers.

THIRD HOUSE: GEMINI. *Thou shalt not take the name of the Lord thy God in vain.* The Third House reveals how one relates himself to his spiritual friends or fellow disciples.

FOURTH HOUSE: CANCER. *Remember the Sabbath Day, to keep it holy.* The Fourth House expresses the etheric body, the vitality, the health, the intuition, the insight. The Fourth House shows the power of Divine Mother in the life of the past and reveals one's reverence. Also, the Fourth House contains the collective debris of the lower Quelle or subconscious.

FIFTH HOUSE: LEO. *Honor thy father and thy mother.* The Fifth House reveals the akasic records dramatized through the Devas' akasic dramas. In the Fifth House may be seen the particular phase of dramatization one will express in the making of his own myths as a self embodied in an ego, playing his part on the stage according to karma or grace. Dramatization of the Ethic falls in the Fifth House. That is how one learns, and where Marking and Tracing are most beneficial.

SIXTH HOUSE: VIRGO. *Thou shalt not kill.* The Sixth House shows how one serves God. The greatest sound, which is the Name-of-God sounding, is *Om*. The Name of God in the chart of each person is indicated in the House of Virgo, where one is led into the Path of Righteousness through the sounding of the OM. The *Name* of God is the Audible Sound; it is the Vibration of God sounding in the Kundalini. On the Kundalini's rising, one experiences God-Realization and is in communion with God.

SEVENTH HOUSE: LIBRA. *Thou shalt not commit adultery.* The Seventh House expresses the physical body and physical works. The Seventh House relates to the keeping of vows in partnership and marriage. If one has Aquarius in the Seventh House, he works for humanity; he is an altruist; he must have a cause to express himself happily.

EIGHTH HOUSE: SCORPIO. *Thou shalt not steal. The tenth shall be holy unto the Lord.* The Eighth House shows the cargo of the soul one brings, the gifts or *Siddhi* powers gained from former lives. The Eighth House is the House of karma, of rebirth; it bears the record of ego-karma.

NINTH HOUSE: SAGITTARIUS. *Thou shalt not bear false witness against thy neighbor.* The Ninth House is the seat of the higher mind. The Ninth House shows one's placement in religion and in soul evolvement.

TENTH HOUSE: CAPRICORN. *Thou shalt not covet.* The Tenth House expresses creation, originality, inventiveness, success. The Tenth House expresses a public life, prominence. It also expresses fame. If it is empty, there is no fame. The Tenth House shows how one will display his gifts, exhibit them or be known for them.

ELEVENTH HOUSE: AQUARIUS. *Love thy neighbor as thyself.* The Eleventh House is the House of the Masters.

The Eleventh House shows how one relates to the Master or Masters.

TWELFTH HOUSE: PISCES. *Thou shalt love the Lord thy God with all thy heart, mind, soul and strength. Love ye one another.* The Twelfth House shows how far one may go into the depth of the collective unconscious and of one's own unconscious.

Place is as important as race. In latitude and longitude placement may be seen the virtue or its lack; virilities earned from past-life polarities or placements may also be seen.

The planets one has on the ascendant in the 12th, the 11th and the 10th Houses indicate the initiation processes of the highest order. This part of the horoscope relates to the Galaxy Gate, or that penetrable portion of the Cosmos Galaxy energies falling into the cosmic eternity-system door or entry.

The heavier diffusions of karma and the way they are transenergized fall into the 7th, 6th, and 5th Houses in the chart. Here, one may see how his karmic burden may be purified and transenergized into light.

The 9th, 8th and 7th Houses indicate what one brings with him as to religious principle and ethic.

The 4th, 3rd and 2nd Houses reveal what one will gain in this life to carry over into his future life as grace or as karma.

The rising sign, or ascendant of a person, is no stronger than his 2nd, 3rd or 4th Houses.

All of the unreachable karma is revealed in the 11th, 10th, 9th, 8th and 7th Houses of the etheric chart.

One's dedication to serve, and his constancy-inclinations to render service, are found in the 6th, 5th, 4th and 3rd Houses.

In the first and second Houses of the etheric chart is found the work one will do in the world to work out his karma.

THE TWELVE ZODIACAL HOUSES AND THEIR INFLUENCES
IN THE PHYSICAL WORLD

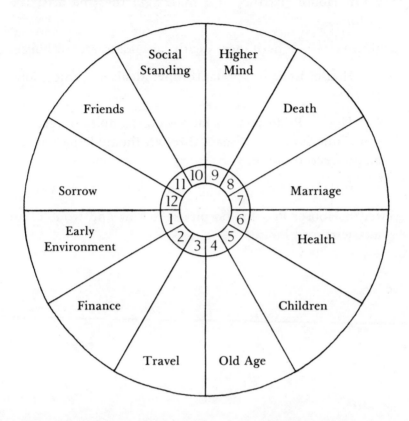

First House: The shape and condition of the body; early environment and childhood home.

Second House: Finance; attitude toward money; stewardship.

Third House: Literature; the useful arts; practical intelligence; short journeys; brothers and sisters.

Fourth House: The home; conditions in old age; inheritance of disease from the female parent; an akasic-record house.

Fifth House: Amusement; courtship; children; speculation.

Sixth House: Health; servants; labor.

Seventh House: Partnership; marriage; the fine arts; the public.

Eighth House: Inheritance; death; an akasic-record house.

Ninth House: Religion; philanthropy; idealism; justice; long journeys.

Tenth House: Profession; social position; ambition; recognition; inheritance of disease through the male parent; an akasic-record house.

Eleventh House: Friends; hopes and wishes; the Masters.

Twelfth House: Prisons; hospitals; sorrow and trouble; an akasic-record house.

Chart: Birth to Consciousness. The knowledge one receives when he opens the energy-processes of the four bodies and transenergizes their vibrations into consciousness:

God
I Am that I Am
Greater Archetypal Cycles
Buddhi as Intellect
Higher Self and Higher Mind
Transcendental Immunity
Power as Emanation
Power as Will
Higher Self-Genesis
Cosmos-Genesis
All-Genesis
One-Genesis

GOD
SPIRIT

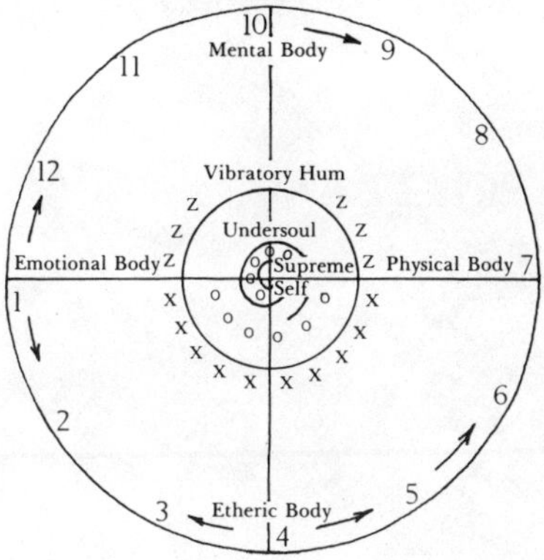
10
Mental Body
9
11
8
12
Vibratory Hum
Undersoul
Emotional Body
Supreme Self
Physical Body
7
1
2
6
5
3
Etheric Body
4

SOUL

Ego Birth-Station
Chitta or Intelligible Life-Stuff
Desire
Motivation and Attentiveness
Concentration
Soul-Record
Self as I
Memory of Desire
Immunity-Astral
Awareness as Conscience
Power as Choice
Power as Authorization
Ego as Intellect
Memory in Possessing Objects
Memory of Race
Appearance—as given from Past-life Chastity or Karmas

EGO

Gene-Inheritance
Objective Awareness
Karmic
Maya
Psychology
Metaphysics
Family
Society
Orthodox Religion
Memory of Association
Insanity and Ignorance
Power as Presentation
Intellect as Family
Memory in Life-Blood and Cells, Tissues
Bio-Genesis
Family-Genesis
Self as Me
● Me and the Other

ANGELS

Angelic and Devas
Vita
Cyclic-Law Energy
Inner-Parts Law
Timing
Miracles and Cycles
Mirror and Chimera
Primordial Akash
Primordial Record
Religiosity
Memory of Cycles, as Forming the Self
Past-Life Memories
Cell-Life as Primordial
Immunity-Bacterial
Immunity-Psychic
Awareness as Inner Power
Awareness as Vitality
Awareness as Duration
Power as Instinct
Power as Intuition
Power as Healing
Self as Imaged of God

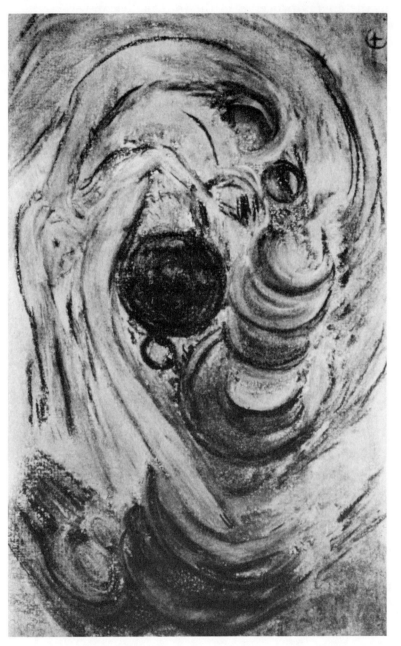

MOVING DEEP

Ann Ree Colton, 1952

Hierarchy: "Let us make man in our image, after our likeness." (Genesis 1:26) Hierarchy and the Father at work. "And the Spirit of God moved upon the face of the waters." (Genesis 1:2)

"Let There Be Light" (Genesis 1:3)

Ann Ree Colton, 1952

The Earth's Nebula Takes Form as She Creates Mars

Ann Ree Colton, 1952

THE EARTH's NEBULA CREATES MERCURY

Ann Ree Colton, 1952

The Earth's Nebula Working with the Shaping of Saturn

Ann Ree Colton, 1952

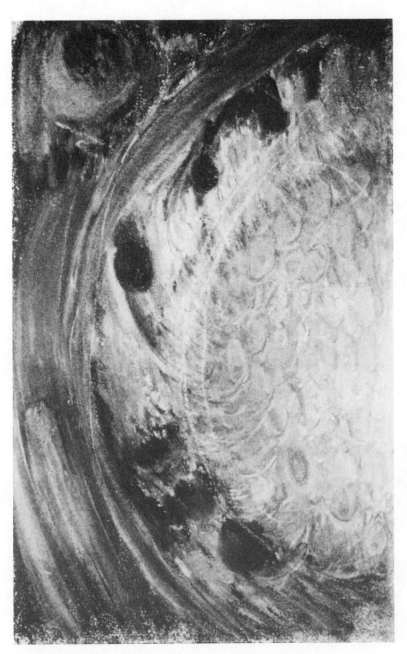

THE FIRST MANIFESTATION OF THE EARTH'S NEBULA AND THE BIRTH OF THE MOON. SEALING IN THE ARCHETYPES

Ann Ree Colton, 1952

93

The Earth's Nebula Works with the Creating of Its Accompanying Planets and Starts Its Cooling Process

Ann Ree Colton, 1952

The Earth's Nebula Creates Jupiter

Ann Ree Colton, 1952

LIGHT-STREAMS BETWEEN GALAXY SYSTEMS THROUGH WHICH THE SOULS OF MEN REINCARNATE THAT THEY MAY CREATE WITH GOD

Ann Ree Colton, 1952

The Sun's Nebula and Stirring of the Atoms in
Creation and Sealing in the Eternal Sustaining Atoms
of Souls to Be Born on the Planet Earth   Ann Ree Colton, 1952

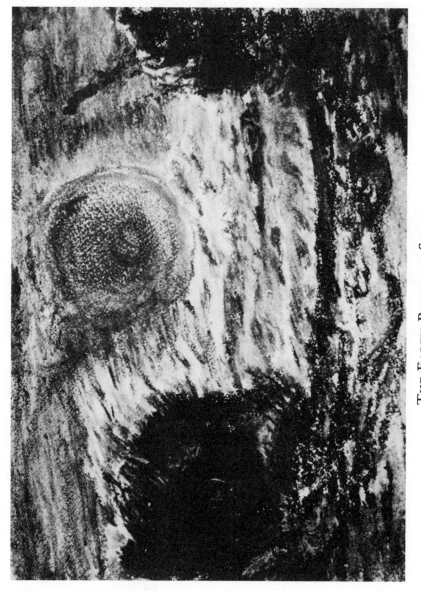

THE EARTH BEGINS TO SOLIDIFY

Ann Ree Colton, 1952

SOUL

The bounds of the soul thou shalt not find, though you travel every way.

> —Heraclitus, 500 B.C.

And I say let a man be of good cheer about his soul. When the soul has been arrayed in her own proper jewels — temperance, and justice, and courage, and nobility and truth — she is ready to go on her journey when the hour comes.

> —Socrates, minutes before
> his execution, 399 B.C.

Of all things which a man has, next to the gods, his soul is the most divine and most truly his own.

> —Plato, 4th Century B.C.

When I reflect on the nature of the soul, it seems to me by far more difficult and obscure to determine its character while it is in the body, a strange domicile, than to imagine what it is when it leaves it, and has arrived in the empyreal regions, in its own and proper home.

> —Cicero, 44 B.C.

God is not only the Creator, but the Country of the soul.

> —St. Augustine, c. 397 A.D.

God first purifies the souls in which He dwells, then He illumines them, and finally leads them to divine union.

> —Dionysius, c. 500 A.D.

The soul is the primary principle of our nourishment, sensation, movement, and understanding.

> —St. Thomas Aquinas, 1272

4

THE GREAT ARCHITECT

*This wonderful ordering of the sun, the
planets and the comets cannot but be the work
of an intelligent, all-powerful Being.*
—Isaac Newton, 1687

SOLAR-SYSTEM MANSIONS

In my Father's house are many mansions.
—St. John 14:2

God, the Great Architect, is designing and creating many
Mansions in His Universe. Each Mansion, or Solar System, is
fulfilling an *Archetypal Design* or *Blueprint* established by
the Intelligence of the Creator. This Blueprint determines the
purposes and goals of each Star.

Stars, Star Clusters, Galaxies and Galaxy Clusters are
governed by a unifying Archetypal Design. Thus, all celestial
bodies work harmoniously within a Cosmos System of progressive purposefulness.

The planet Earth is an essential part of the overall Creation of the Universe. The Archetypal Design for the Sun, the
Planets and their Moons determines their movement-cycles,
velocities, and directions.

101

God builds each Mansion or Solar System as an individual structure that blends with all other Solar Mansions in the Universe. Even as a wise architect designs a building with great care and creativity, and supervises each detail during the actual construction, so does the Great Architect establish the blueprints for each stage of the creation of a Solar System. The essential building materials and the skilled craftsmen are provided by the Wisdom of God — and work proceeds under His careful supervision.

No thing and no one can keep a Solar System from fulfilling the Blueprint Design of the Creator. Those who are privileged to work directly with God in His architectural masterpieces are the Prophets, the Saints, the Sages and other disciplined and enlightened personages. The Christ, as the Architect's Chief Assistant, assures that all progress is in exact accord with the Blueprint envisioned by the Beautiful Intelligence of God.

Each Solar System in the Universe has its unique Blueprint that determines its size, magnitude of light, and creation-cycles. Each Solar System is under the constant direction of the Omnipresent Architect and His *masterbuilders.*

> *According to the grace of God which is given unto me, as a wise masterbuilder, I have laid the foundation, and another buildeth thereon.*
> *—1 Corinthians 3:10*

Each person on Earth is seeking to become a masterbuilder for God. Trusted and trustworthy masterbuilders work with God every day in every way. These dedicated craftsmen are the *Elect* who have attained a love-union with the Will of God. Centered in God's Will, the Elect work knowingly and joyfully with the Blueprint determining each step and stage of the creation of the Solar System.

A sacramental love for God based upon daily worship-dedications keeps the heart and mind ever-ready to heed the

Courtesy of Virgil Smith and Silas Elash.

Divine Will. Faith in the perfection, power and majesty of God unites one with the sacred company of the Elect. Gradually, knowledge and understanding are gained through close association with the enlightened souls entrusted by the Creator to do His Will.

> *Behold my servant, whom I uphold; mine elect,*
> *in whom my soul delighteth; I have put my spirit*
> *upon him.*
>
> *—Isaiah 42:1*

The Intelligence of God within the Archetypal Blueprint of the Sun and its planets is present in every atom. The Intelligence of God is nonrecognizable by the human spirit during certain stages of life on Earth. As the intelligence of man matures through natural growth processes, he begins to discern a Greater Intelligence than his own limited capacity for comprehension. When an individual reaches the time when he desires to work directly with the Great Architect, he has reached a stage of evolutionary achievement that moves his heart and mind beyond the barriers separating Heaven and Earth.

In the Archetypal Design for the planet Earth, God has provided an accompanying *Heaven* where reside Beings and Presences with an intelligence greater than the present intelligence of man. These Beings and Presences, dwelling in Heaven's light, are invisible to physical sight; their sanctified intelligence is used by God to assist Him in the creation of the Solar System as a whole and in the creation of each individual experiencing life on Earth.

The Archetypal Design for each Star is protected from any form of intrusion. The Archetype is surrounded by an energy-sea of fiery intensity. Purity is an essential virtue for anyone who would read the Scroll of Archetypal Truths regarding his Solar-System home. Therefore, all enlightened sages and holy personages direct their proteges to purify their hearts, minds and souls.

When mankind as a whole desires to fulfill the Archetypal Design of its own Solar-System home, the Door will open to the knowledge of the Archetypes of brother and sister Stars. Before this ordained occurrence becomes a reality, the human spirit must first learn the importance of morality, ethic, righteousness, love and law.

The *integrity* of each Archetype in the starry Universe is self-protecting and self-fulfilling. The integrity of one Archetype is communicable to the integrity of another Archetype. Man may discover and discern the key to comprehending the Universal Archetypes only through his own expression of integrity.

> *And as for me, thou upholdest me in mine integrity, and settest me before thy face for ever.*
> *—Psalm 41:12*

The Sacred Scriptures counsel man to express the virtue of integrity in all of his associations with his fellow man and in his relationship with God; for, through integrity, the intelligence of man fuses and blends with the Intelligence of God. In this, one is endowed with the Gifts of Wisdom and Understanding, Reverence and Love. Such purified souls then may work daily with the Intelligence of God as it guides their course, enlightens their minds, and expands their love.

The enlightened state of an ethical and moral intelligence unites one with the Beings and Presences of Higher Intelligence in the Heavens that are part of this Solar System. The work of these Illumined Beings is to prepare the human spirit to learn about the Archetypes of other Star Systems. This next step in evolution will be accomplished through an integrity in harmony with the Intelligence of Omnipresent God.

As men on Earth practice the wise principles espoused by Jesus, they will learn that these principles are, in reality, *Cosmos Principles*. Cosmos Principles are keys to the Code of the Universe. Through the Cosmos Principles being planted as seeds in men's hearts and minds, Jesus is preparing the human spirit to transcend the bewildering complexities of life on Earth and to discover the simplicity-logics of the Code of Cosmos. With the Saints and other Holy Personages as their inspired guides, men on Earth are moving gradually toward a comprehension of this unifying Code.

The advent of modern-day astronomy has introduced the strong possibility that numerous Solar Systems in the Universe contain human life and intelligence. This assumption is based upon the logic of mathematical probability. Daily, astronomers and radio-astronomers are seeking to discover the Code that will unlock the door to communication with other inhabitants of the Cosmos.

Love is the major key to decoding the Cosmos Code. The Intelligence of God everywhere present in the Universe reveals its secrets and mysteries only where love is pure, selfless, reverent and constant. Thus, the Enlightened Teachers of all religious philosophies emphasize the importance of love.

The higher degrees of love are not easily attainable. The diversions and pleasures of life, the pitfalls of pride, and the shadows of prejudice interfere with the mind stillness and heart purity necessary for communion with the Intelligence of God. With the key of love, the Code of God's Omnipresent Intelligence begins to reveal its secret splendors and unifying Constants.

Each Constant ascertained by science heralds an important breakthrough in comprehending the Code of Cosmos. In 1926, when the speed of light was discovered to be a Universal Constant, mankind began its ascendency toward the Throne of Divinity. The "many mansions" mentioned by Jesus were no longer an unsolvable mystery. The knowledge of the speed and spectrum of light placed the human spirit into the hard-won position of perceiving and utilizing a *Constant* shared by all other Stars and Galaxies in the Universe. The energy-code of Cosmos began to be solved: a code of color, tone, cycle and symbol.

> *The most incomprehensible thing about the universe is that it is comprehensible.*
>   —*Albert Einstein*

THE IMAGE-OF-GOD CONSTANT

> *So God created man in his own image, in the image of God created he him; male and female created he them.*
>   —*Genesis 1:27*

Even as there is a Blueprint for the creation of each individual Solar System, so is there a Master Blueprint for each Cluster of Stars and for each Cluster of Galaxies. The overall Creation of the Universe has One All-encompassing Blueprint called *the Image of God*. Each and every Soul, Star and Galaxy is part of this Master Blueprint for All Creation, past, present and future.

The Image of God is Constant throughout the Universe. As a Universal Constant, the Image of God unites all *consciousness beings* in all Worlds, Kingdoms, Stars and Galaxies.

In each Solar System, specific facets of God's Image are being emphasized by those assigned to that particular Star-Mansion. A facet of God's Image may require milleniums before it begins to reveal its Splendor; a facet of God's Image may require sojourns in numerous Solar Systems before it begins to reveal its Glory. One by one, the facets of God's Image come forth as scintillating facets of a Dimensional Diamond. The Eternal Diamond of God's Dimensionality contains multitudinous facets of Grace and Truth.

"One star differeth from another star in glory." (1 Corinthians 15:41) The glory of one Star is a mighty Archetypal facet of God's Omnipresent Diamond. To learn of the supernal glory of one Star is to learn of Eternal Constants, Universal Laws and Cosmos Principles ever-present in all starry creations. Thus, the scientific-spiritual approach to the Altar of God on Earth leads one to the Altar of God in the Cosmos. The Stars, as lighted candles on the Altar of Cosmos, reveal their secrets to the reverent heart and dedicated mind. The marriage of the scientific and the spiritual within one's being signifies a new and greater participation with God in His creation of Man, the Stars, the Galaxies, the Universe.

Each of us possesses a soul, but we do not prize our souls as creatures made in God's image deserve, and so we do not understand the great secrets which they contain.

—St. Teresa of Avila, 1577

The soul, when it shall have driven away from itself all that is contrary to the divine will, becomes transformed in God by love.

—St. John of the Cross, c. 1584

TIME AND TIMELESSNESS

And the angel which I saw stand upon the sea and upon the earth lifted up his hand to the heaven, And sware by him that liveth for ever and ever, who created heaven, and the things that therein are, and the earth, and the things that therein are, and the sea, and the things that are therein, that there should be time no longer.

—*Revelation 10:5,6*

The numerous dimensions of God's Spirit range from the mansions of Time to the mansions of Timelessness. The five senses register the mansions of Time through the visible cycles of the Sun, the Moon and the Earth. However, the more one contemplates the reality of the Soul, the more he gains access to the dimensions or mansions of Timelessness.

"Seek ye first the Kingdom of God, and His righteousness." *(St. Matthew 6:33)* Each Heaven within the Kingdom of God is a mansion of Timeless Truths and Infinite degrees of Grace.

A scientist becomes a spiritual initiate after he begins to experience his soul and its broad spectrum of dimensionality. A spiritual initiate becomes a scientist who investigates works in the laboratory of the soul. Thereafter, God—as Physical Truth and Spiritual Truth—may reveal His Spirit within Time and within Timelessness.

A scientist open to God's Intelligence becomes a *prophet* in his discipline—for the nature of God's Intelligence is Pure

Prophecy revealed through the overcoming of Time. Such scientists have gained a glimpse of the Archetypal Blueprint of the creation of the Earth. Each perception of the Blueprint of the Earth's creation is a visitation by God's Spirit beyond Time and Space.

The Gift of Illumination enables one to work in a sustained union with the Eternal Spirit of God. To earn this priceless Gift, one first must be initiated in the secrets of Time and Timelessness. Time and Timelessness represent different wavelengths within the Spectrum of Truth.

The scientific study of Time leads to new understanding of the nature of the Universe. The spiritual comprehension of Time's overcoming enables one to work in the world as a Prophet and Revelator for God.

Each mansion of Time and each mansion of Timelessness contains many lessons necessary for the enlightenment of the human spirit. The senses, when disciplined and reverent, lead to the soul. The soul, in turn, prepares one to experience an illumined knowledge of Time and Timelessness.

The language of the soul is a Cosmos-Eternal Language. The Constants of God are the soul's language. Wherever the soul is sent by the Creator to experience life in the Universe, the One Language of God's Constants is spoken and understood. It remains for the heart and mind to become knowledgeable in the soul's language. Through the Constants of God manifesting through symbols, cycles, colors and tones, the soul is in a perpetual state of learning and of contributing to the Creation of the Cosmos.

The Tower-of-Babel era caused men to be separated by different languages. The language of love will gradually remove all language-barriers. When this occurs, all peoples in the world will communicate through one language. The confusion and separation caused by numerous languages will be healed and overcome through Love. When the language of love unites man with the soul's language of Eternal Constants, he will work directly with the Great Architect and His mighty Blueprints of Creation.

GALAXY COVENANTS

All the paths of the Lord are mercy and truth
unto such as keep his covenant and his testimonies.
                              —*Psalm 25:10*

The Universe is being created through a system of *Covenants*: Solar-System Covenants, Star-Cluster Covenants, Galaxy Covenants and Galaxy-Cluster Covenants. These Covenants determine the birth, purpose and ending of each Star, Star Cluster, Galaxy and Galaxy Cluster.

Each Solar System is part of a *Galaxy Covenant*. Each Galaxy is part of a *Galaxy-Cluster Covenant*. These Covenants may extend for many billions of years. Each Galaxy-Cluster Covenant and the Covenant of each individual Galaxy within the Cluster blend with the Covenants of all other Stars and Galaxies.

Every inch of Space through which a Galaxy or Star moves is determined by its Covenant. Every atom of energy necessary for the birth, life and death of a Star, Star Cluster, Galaxy or Galaxy Cluster is determined by its Covenant.

All Galaxy Covenants are accomplished through the Archetypes or Blueprints of the Great Architect. The Archetypes of a Galaxy Cluster may be likened to the master blueprints for the building of a Cathedral. The Master Architect and His Son are constructing the Cathedral of Cosmos through the Greater-Covenant Blueprints. Hosts of Beings and Presences work with God and the Christ in the everlasting creation of Stars and Galaxies. Through Covenants and Archetypes, the Plan proceeds to unfold. Man becomes a conscious part of the Creation of the Universe the moment he begins to think in terms of Covenants and Archetypes.

The Covenant of any celestial body in the Cosmos is an Immutable Truth. No one or thing can intrude upon the Covenant. The Intelligence of God is present each moment in every aspect of the Covenant regarding a Galaxy, a Star or a Soul.

SOUL-COVENANTS

> *The secret of the Lord is with them that fear him; and he will shew them his covenant.*
> —*Psalm 25:14*

The Soul works with and through Covenants with God. The Soul, as a Cosmos Voyager, establishes a Covenant with God upon entering a Solar System. This Covenant determines the degrees of light and love the Soul will contribute to the Creation of the Solar System, the Galaxy, the Galaxy Cluster and the Universe.

The Soul's Covenant with God is an integral part of the Solar-System Covenant, the Galaxy Covenant and the Galaxy-Cluster Covenant. All Covenants are the Will of God—therefore, the Universe is one of Total Harmony at all times.

True physical and spiritual happiness begins when one desires to work within the wisdom and beauty of his Soul's Covenant with God. The willingness to fulfill the Soul's Covenant with the Creator moves one into the harmony-flow of the Universe. The harmony-flow places one in timing with the Cycles of his Soul, the Cycles of the Solar System and the Cycles of the Milky Way Galaxy. To be in timing with God's Creation of the Galaxies is joy indescribable, for one is in perfect harmony with the overall Creation of the Universe.

*He that getteth wisdom loveth his own soul: he
that keepeth understanding shall find good.*
                                        —Proverbs 19:8

A person may be ego-centered or soul-centered. Ego-centered persons resist God and His Wisdom. Such persons are as a space capsule drifting without a compass, a gyroscope, a direction or a destination.

To be soul-centered is to receive the Wisdom of the Soul's Covenant, which is an *Eternal Wisdom*. Union with the Soul's Covenant is the beginning of a life of Grace. Gratitude for the Soul and its Covenant unites one with the Grace of God's Wisdom and Love.

The Soul's Wisdom is the sum total of all the Wisdom one has gained in past lives on Earth and in other Solar-System Mansions; it also includes the Wisdom gained in all other planes, spheres, realms and dimensional kingdoms accessible to the Soul. This vast storehouse of Wisdom opens increasingly to the humble, the righteous, the reverent and the just. The Soul's Wisdom gained through experience leads naturally to union with deeper levels of God's Wisdom through sacramental attitudes and virtues.

The Soul, being of God, is filled with the Knowledge of God and His Kingdoms. Through Soul-Covenant Wisdom, one experiences the Glory of God within His Kingdoms.

An Anointed Teacher of Truth, expressing his Soul's Covenant with God, is filled with the Wisdom inspired by the Soul and the Creator. When a seeker after Truth desires to fulfill his Soul's Covenant with God, his Teacher opens to him the priceless riches of the Soul. As the Soul's Wisdom of the seeker increases in his being, the Soul's Covenant presents its treasures of Truth, Beauty and Grace.

It is holy joy to be at one with the Soul's Covenant from life to life. However, before this joy may fill one's being, he must yearn to blend his will with God's Will. The Mediation of Jesus accelerates the union of the individual's will with God's Will, thereby blessing one with the Soul's Wisdom and Divine Wisdom.

The Soul's Wisdom inspires one to fulfill God's Laws. This, in turn, unites one with the Wisdom of God within His Laws. Thus, Soul-Wisdom expressed by the heart and mind qualifies one for union with God's Wisdom within His Laws and Commandments. The result of this sacred fusion between Soul-Wisdom and God's Wisdom is *Enlightenment*. *"The statutes of the Lord are right, rejoicing the heart: the commandment of the Lord is pure, enlightening the eyes." (Psalm 19:8)*

The human soul is a silent harp in God's quire, whose strings need only to be swept by the divine breath to chime in with the harmonies of creation.
— Henry David Thoreau, 1838

Nothing can be greater than it . . . It is wider than space, older than time, wide as hope, rich as love.
— Ralph Waldo Emerson, 1849

Close by the rights of man, side by side with them, are the rights of the soul.
— Victor Hugo, 1862

I affirm that there is a power in the Soul which is unmoved by time or the flesh: this power floweth from the Spirit, yet abideth therein. Yea, it is all spirit.
— Meister Eckhart, 1260?–1327?

PENALTIES AND REWARDS

> *He that receiveth a prophet in the name of a*
> *prophet shall receive a prophet's reward; and he*
> *that receiveth a righteous man in the name of a*
> *righteous man shall receive a righteous man's*
> *reward.*
>
> —*St. Matthew 10:41*

Each soul living on Earth has *covenanted* with God to inhabit a Solar System based upon the Principle of Penalties and Rewards. When the Holy Laws governing life on Earth are offended, penalties are exacted. When the Holy Laws are fulfilled, rewards are earned.

The penalties and rewards experienced by one in each lifetime are determined by the Perfect Justice of God. The goal of the soul is to inspire the heart and mind to utilize *free will* as an instrument of love, law and creation so that one may be free from penalties and receive the multitudinous rewards that constitute a *State of Grace*.

"Love is the fulfilling of the law." (Romans 13:10) Grace results from a love-fulfillment of the law. A perpetual State of Grace is attainable through the continuous observance of Holy Law. The wise live under the ever-flowing waterfall of God's Grace. The unenlightened are not yet motivated to live according to sacred statutes and covenants; therefore, they remain subject to the penalties of pain and suffering.

"Of a truth I perceive that God is no respecter of persons." *(Acts 10:34)* The Holy Laws of God are as *impersonal* as the Law of Gravity or the Law of Electromagnetism. If one wittingly or unwittingly offends the Law of Gravity, he experiences a painful penalty: a bruise, a broken limb, or death caused by a fall. The same principle holds true for any failure to observe Holy Law.

Free will united with Holy Law is a time of rejoicing for the soul, for one is then free to receive the rewards that ennoble life on Earth and contribute to the creation of the Cosmos. The soul is at home in any sphere, plane, world or dimension in Cosmos. The rewards visited upon the heart and mind include the knowledge of the Eternal nature of the soul and the Cosmos capabilities of the soul. Once the soul is *free* through free will united with Holy Law, one perceives the Wisdom and Mercy of God within penalties and the Love and Grace of God within rewards.

> *For the Son of man shall come in the glory of his Father with his angels; and then he shall reward every man according to his works.*
> —*St. Matthew 16:27*

The soul of a nation is the composite of all souls dwelling in the nation. The soul of each nation has a covenant with the Creator based upon its Archetype. As long as the nation fulfills its Archetypal Covenant—the reason for its being—the blessings of God remain with the people to guide, inspire and protect them. If the citizens of a nation forsake God and His Laws, the nation is no longer graced with protection. Such nations remain exposed to "wars and rumours of wars." (St. Matthew 24:6)   Poverty, misery and fear visit a nation that strays from its covenant with God.

Each race of peoples has its covenant with God. Every religion has its covenant with God. Every family has its covenant with God. Wherever there are individuals, groups or masses of people, there are Archetypal Covenants with God. The rewards of happiness and the penalties of unhappiness experienced by a person, family, religion, nation or race are determined by the covenants and their fulfillment or nonfulfillment.

> . . . *when Thy judgments are in the earth, the inhabitants of the world will learn righteousness.*
> —*Isaiah 26:9*

THE GREATER COVENANTS

> *But the mercy of the Lord is from everlasting to*
> *everlasting upon them that fear him, and his*
> *righteousness unto children's children; To such as*
> *keep his covenant and to those that remember his*
> *commandments to do them.*
> —*Psalm 103:17,18*

The Scriptural references to the Creator and His children pertain to the keeping of the Ten Commandments. The knowledge of other Covenants opens to man as he applies the moral, ethical and spiritual principles within the Ten Commandments.

The *Divine-Image Covenant* is an Eternal Covenant between God and Man.

The *Cosmos Covenant* is between God and all Stars and Galaxies in the Universe.

A *Galaxy-Cluster Covenant* is between God and the Galaxies within a cluster of Galaxies.

A *Galaxy Covenant* is between God and the Stars within each individual Galaxy.

A *Star-Cluster Covenant* is between God and the Stars within a Cluster of Stars.

A *Solar-System Covenant* is the Covenant between God and each individual Solar System.

The *Soul's Covenant* is between God and each living Soul. The Reincarnation-Cycles experienced by the Soul in a Solar System are determined by the Soul's Covenant with God.

The Divine-Image Covenant and the Soul's Covenant determine the Solar System, the Star Cluster, the Galaxy and the Galaxy Cluster in which the Soul will experience Life and Learning.

Jesus . . . the mediator of the new covenant.
—Hebrews 12:24

The knowledge sealed into the Earth by the Lord Jesus pertains to the beginning of the New Covenant. The New Covenant is preparing man for the time when he will work willingly and knowingly with God on broader ranges of action and service. In this, he will become cognizant of his Soul's Covenant, the Divine-Image Covenant, the Solar-System Covenant, the Star-Cluster Covenant, the Galaxy-Covenant, the Galaxy-Cluster Covenant and the Cosmos Covenant.

Keep therefore the words of this covenant, and
do them, that ye may prosper in all that ye do.
—Deuteronomy 29:9

THE COMMANDMENT OF LIFE EVERLASTING

The Father which sent me, he gave me a commandment, what I should say, and what I should speak. And I know that his commandment is life everlasting.
—St. John 12:49,50

The Image of God is an *Eternal Image* manifesting through the Commandment of Life Everlasting. As man evolves spiritually, he discovers the Covenants and Commandments that determine his Eternal-Image destiny in the Universe.

Until recent decades, mankind thought of its existence in terms of *thousands* of years. The advent of new scientific knowledge presented evidence of man inhabiting the planet Earth for *millions* of years. The future holds the promise of man's thinking of his existence in terms of *billions* of years. In time, the knowledge of Eternal Life as a Universal Truth

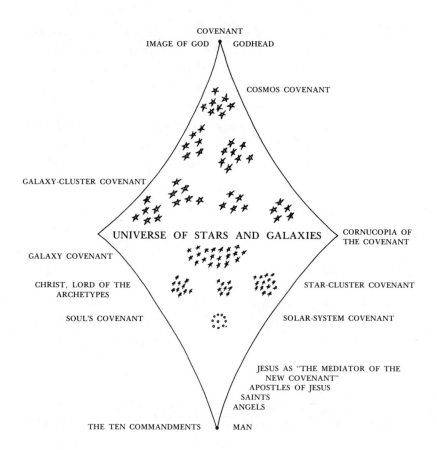

THE GREATER COVENANTS

as well as a Spiritual Commandment will be acknowledged by the consciousness mind of man. When this occurs, the human spirit will respond willingly to the Image of God, which works through Covenants involving Cycles of countless billions of years.

The *Divine-Image Covenant* pertains to *series* of life-cycles experienced by the soul in a number of Solar Systems within the Galaxies. The *Soul's Covenant* relates to series of one's lives in a specific Solar System. The Divine-Image Covenant is an Everlasting Covenant between the individual and God. This ongoing Covenant occurs in segments of hundreds of billions of years. The Soul's Covenant extends for the life-cycle of a single Star, depending on the size and life-duration of the Star.

Man's present comprehension of *Time* is limited. What man thinks of as billions of years seems to him a lengthy period of Time. In the Eternals, untold billions of years are necessary to accomplish the long-range purposes of God's Will.

Upon one's uniting with the Soul's Covenant, the door opens to his comprehension of the Divine-Image Covenant. The Christ *is* this Door—thus, when one serves God in the *Name* of His Son, knowledge increases regarding the Soul and the Divine Image.

Through Soul-Realization, one learns of the Soul's Covenant. Through God-Realization, he learns of the Divine-Image Covenant.

> *And the Lord God formed man of the dust of the ground, and breathed into his nostrils the breath of life; and man became a living soul.*
> —Genesis 2:7

The Eternal Image of God is within every living soul— therefore, the soul is Eternal. The Image of God and the soul work through the Holy Law of Reincarnation. This mighty Law enables the soul to continuously manifest new facets of the Divine Image during lengthy periods of learning in Solar Systems and in Galaxies. Through the Law of Reincarnation, the soul of each person on Earth preserves the essences of the experiences and lessons learned from birth to death in each lifetime. From life to life, the reincarnating soul gathers essences and quintessences of knowledge, wisdom and truth.

The Image of God in the soul determines where and when one lives in the Universe: the Galaxy he will inhabit; the Sun that will welcome him; and the planet that will house him. After the Sun concludes its life-span, the Image of God will determine the placement of the soul and its reincarnation life-rhythms within a new Solar-System home.

Man learns slowly. He learns at a tempo or timing determined by the faculties and opportunities provided by the Divine Image.

If the Divine Image places the soul in a primitive tribe, one will learn very slowly. Primitive tribes may be one's home for hundreds of lifetimes. However, each life will provide necessary lesson-essences that will prepare the reincarnating soul for a broader range of knowledge, wisdom and truth.

Presently, the reincarnating soul is gaining important lessons through lives in families, races and nations. Gradually, the consciousness mind of each individual is being prepared to learn about, and to work with, the Soul's Covenant and the Divine-Image Covenant. This inevitable moment in Time and Space will occur either in the present Solar System or in a future Solar System.

The Divine-Image Covenant and the Soul's Covenant are one — however, before one may begin to ascertain the Divine-Image Covenant, he must first learn of his Soul and its Covenant with God. Even as the consciousness mind and heart eventually will know the soul to be an immortal and eternal reality, so will the knowledge of the Divine Image be a solid foundation-truth upon which one will build from life to life.

"*I am the door.*" *(St. John 10:9)* Jesus is the door to the Glory and Splendor of God within the soul and the Divine Image. The Divine Image is one's link with every Star and Galaxy being created in the Universe.

Through the Mediation of Jesus, one learns first of his Soul-Self, and next he learns of his Divine-Image Self. Knowledge of the soul discloses cardinal truths about the Soul's Covenant. Knowledge about the Image of God produces mighty breakthroughs in understanding the Divine-Image Covenant.

> *Ye were as sheep going astray; but are now returned unto the Shepherd and Bishop of your souls.*
> —2 Peter 2:25

The Wisdom of Jesus contains the formulas for freedom from all forms of bondages. The greatness of Jesus in the sight of God is beyond man's present comprehension. The greatness of Jesus enables Him to open every door to the mysteries and secrets of the Cosmos. To live under the Mantle of Jesus' Love and Wisdom is to be blessed with increasing knowledge of the wondrous Plan of Eternal Life.

> *Whenever one gives a testimony to the Covenant of God, he unites with the Power of the Universe.*

THE MIRACLES OF MOSES AND JESUS

> *Miracles are not contrary to nature but only contrary to what we know about nature.*
> —Saint Augustine

The miracles of Moses and the miracles of Jesus testify to their knowledge of laws and principles unknown to others.

Moses and Jesus were great spiritual-scientists with advanced wisdom. To become at one with the wisdom of Moses and Jesus is to learn of the laws and principles that produce miracles.

The laws and principles utilized by Moses and Jesus are *basic* truths of the Universe and the Image of God. Every seeker after Truth who looks through the Wisdom-Telescopes of Moses and Jesus sees clearly the Image of God in the Cosmos and in the heart.

> *And the cloud departed from off the tabernacle; and, behold, Miriam became leprous, white as snow: and Aaron looked upon Miriam, and, behold, she was leprous. And Moses cried unto the Lord, saying, Heal her now, O God, I beseech thee.*
> *—Numbers 12:10,13*

Moses revealed the mighty power of God working through him when Miriam was healed of leprosy. The ability to restore a sick or afflicted person to normal health through a miracle reveals that one has wittingly or unwittingly utilized basic spiritual laws and ethics related to Time and the Image of God.

As Messiah, Jesus came to open mankind's understanding of the greater mysteries and secrets of Time and the Image of God. The appointed and Anointed Apostles of Jesus are Prophets due to their ability to overcome the Time-barrier; and they are Revelators because of their knowledge of the Divine Image.

> *And the children of Israel did eat manna forty years, until they came to a land inhabited; they did eat manna, until they came unto the borders of the land of Canaan.*
> *—Exodus 16:35*

The miracles of Moses manifesting in the sight of the Pharaoh freed his people who had suffered four-hundred years of slavery in Egypt. Historians estimate that between 600,000 to 2 million Hebrews followed Moses into the desert. The miracle of feeding this multitude each day for forty years in the parched wilderness reveals the greatness of Moses and his closeness to God. The miracle of the manna provided more than total physical nourishment; the miracle of the manna fed the *faith* of the people, assuring them of God's sure and caring Love.

> *And he commanded the multitude to sit down on the grass, and took the five loaves, and the two fishes, and looking up to heaven, he blessed, and brake, and gave the loaves to his disciples, and the disciples to the multitude. And they did all eat, and were filled: and they took up of the fragments that remained twelve baskets full. And they that had eaten were about five thousand men, beside women and children.*
>
> *—St. Matthew 14:19–21*

The miracle of Jesus feeding thousands of people fishes and loaves of bread reveals His knowledge of holy laws of multiplication and manifestation. Jesus took a few fishes and loaves of bread and multiplied them into thousands of fishes and loaves. Man calls this a "miracle"—however, Jesus used the power of love to manifest fish from fish and bread from bread.

The *image* of fish and the *image* of the grain producing bread have their origins in the Godhead. Jesus' union with the Godhead enabled Him to multiply the image of the fish and the grain. His knowledge of Time and Timelessness enabled Him to accelerate the atom-processes through which an image envisioned by God is manifested on the physical planes.

From former Stars new Stars are formed. From the original fishes and loaves, new fishes and loaves were produced by Jesus. Stars multiply in accordance with the mathematics of the Universe as ordained by God. The core of a Star's atom is Pure Spirit; the core of an atom in a fish or in a seed of grain is Pure Spirit. Jesus, at one with God's Pure Spirit, had command of the atom-energies issuing from Pure Spirit. Thus, the ability of Jesus to image, manifest, quicken and multiply the atoms within the fishes and the loaves produced a memorable miracle.

> *Verily, verily, I say unto you, He that believeth on me, the works that I do shall he do also; and greater works than these shall he do; because I go unto my Father.*
>
> *—St. John 14:12*

Jesus prophesied that men would do "greater works" than His own mighty miracles. When men have attained their true statures as sons of God, they, too, will have the power of miracles on Cosmic *and* Cosmos levels. No longer limited by the slower Time-Cycles, they will work with the quickening light of the Godhead and the Archetypal Light of Pure Truth. Man, as a son of God, will work with the imaging, manifesting and multiplying of Stars and Galaxies. The Miracle of the Fishes and the Loaves was the *beginning* of a new era of understanding of atoms, energies, light, Time and Truth.

Presently, man is capable of multiplying a wide range of blessings through love. With the key of love in his hand, the door of miracles will open and reveal the splendor of simplicity-formulas through which God images, magnifies and multiplies.

> *For the law was given by Moses, but grace and truth came by Jesus Christ.*
>
> *—St. John 1:17*

POINTS OF CONTACT

Stars and Galaxies

Jesus as the Point of
   Contact between Cosmos
   and the Human Spirit

Sun, Moon, Planets,
   Earthlings

The Intelligence of God establishes *Points of Contact* throughout His Universe. Each Galaxy Cluster has its Point of Contact. Each individual Galaxy has its Point of Contact. Each Star has its Point of Contact.

The Lord Jesus is the Point of Contact between the Universe and the Solar System containing the planet Earth. Jesus, as the Mediator, is the Point of Contact between each soul on Earth and the Intelligence of God in the Cosmos Sea of Stars and Galaxies.

The Lord Jesus' *Presence* in the Solar System is the Point of Contact between the Godhead and mankind. The Image of God is centered in the Godhead; therefore, the Image of God in the soul of each person also works as his Point of Contact with the Universe. The Lord Jesus as a Point of Contact and the Divine Image as a Point of Contact work in unison.

The Image of God is man's link with all that *Is*. God as

Omnipresence works through His Image. Man is a Divine Creation of God through the Divine Image. The Presence of Jesus as the Point of Contact between God and Man is awakening in Truth-seeking souls the grandeur, beauty and purposes of the Divine Image.

The Image of God is the Point of Contact from Soul to Soul. The Image of God is the Point of Contact between the Past, the Present and the Future. The Image of God is the Point of Contact between Heaven and Earth.

The uniqueness of each individual is sealed into the Divine Image within the core of his being. Thus, the more one expresses the Image of God, the more he expresses his spiritual uniqueness.

The Lord Jesus blesses, heals, anoints and enlightens through the Image of God in a devotee. The Divine Image is the Point of Contact between the individual and Jesus.

Cosmos wavelengths of telepathy are received by the Divine Image in one's being. During sacramental meditation, the Divine Image becomes the antenna for Cosmos wavelengths of telepathy. In moments of Illumination, Cosmos Truths move telepathically into one's heart, mind and soul — and he *understands* mighty wisdom-truths regarding the Cosmos; the laws and principles governing the Creation of the Universe are perceived with clarity and comprehension.

"For the Son of man is Lord even of the sabbath day." *(St. Matthew 12:8)* The Sabbath Day is the Point of Contact between the Time-Cycles of the planet Earth and the Time-Cycles of the Stars and Galaxies. The Sabbath Day, a "perpetual covenant" (Exodus 31:16) between God and man, provides powerful energies that unite the reverent worshipper with the Wisdom of the Creator.

The quickening of the soul and the Divine Image occurs from Sabbath to Sabbath. Jesus, as the Lord of the Sabbath, *lifts* the soul to heights of spiritual ecstasy and knowledge, thereby enabling the servant of God to perceive and to experience the ascending steps to God's Glory within His Image and within the Universe. *"And I, if I be lifted up from the earth, will draw all men unto me." (St. John 12:32)*

The Eternal Image of God is the Point of Contact between all Heavens, all Universes, all Beings, all Souls. All degrees and dimensions of Divine-Image Illuminations occur through the Lord Jesus—the Point of Contact consecrated by Almighty God. Blessed is he who receives Divine-Image Inspirations, Realizations and Revelations, for he is at one with God and His Beloved Son.

> *Now the Lord is that Spirit: and where the Spirit of the Lord is, there is liberty. But we all, with open face beholding as in a glass the glory of the Lord, are changed into the same image from glory to glory even as by the Spirit of the Lord.*
> *—2 Corinthians 3:17,18*

5

THE LAW OF CYCLES

God builds everything in order through Cycles and Rhythms.

UNIVERSAL AND ARCHETYPAL CYCLES

In Omnipresence cyclic Law, God as Law reproduces Himself in the human realm by and through cyclic repetition. Perfection abides within the Law of God's Increase and expresses itself as perfected consciousness.

When a shift in Galaxy occurs, the Great Unconscious simultaneously produces an Archetypal ripeness. This Archetypal ripeness changes the gravity density obstructing soul and outer consciousness.

A shift in Galaxy produces an *Archetypal Cycle*. During this time, there is a greater expansion in spiritual enlightenment and revelation. Such periods wipe out ignorance, and may be compared to the rising of the Universal Sun, whereby the Universe and man have entered another Day, a Day of expanded consciousness. In these times, the Archetypes distribute the Great Light falling into the minds and lives of those ready for enlightenment.

Accompanying each Archetypal Cycle and Galaxy shift is the changing of the rotational theme in planetary bodies. The obscuring primal-veils veiling away planetary knowledge are lifted; man opens interterrestrial knowledge regarding the Solar System he inhabits.

There are miniature cycles, major cycles and mighty cycles. The Archetypal cyclic flow works with all of these. New and virginal Archetypal beginnings are the result of miniature, major and mighty cycles coinciding or working simultaneously to bring birth to more in consciousness. In no other way may man leap over the scales of the units of measure.

Man in Maya is organized to live an enclosure existence. Freedom from these enclosures, which confine him to the belief in limitation, must come upon him involuntarily as being outside of himself or his own control.

If one lives consciously within the Archetypes, he is in the Great Rhythm; his cycles move faster, and any alien body is discarded and removed. In the Great Rhythm, there are Cycles of which men are unaware. In their tamasic and rajasic natures, they cannot register the velocity of these Cycles.

During Universal initiatory cycles for the masses of peoples, Omnipresence, through the Divine-Companion Presences, moves the seer or prophet beyond the gross cycles. The seer is attuned to the Omni-Dimensional Cycles which are the refined Intelligible, Universal Creations. This is what happens when one becomes a prophet for the Archangels.

One must come into rhythm with the Universal to master the cycles. Through devotional and spiritual practices, one takes hold of the rhythm controlling the greater cycles. By this, he frees his cycles and lives in his true units of measure.

To move with the rhythm of the Cycle of Meditation, the Cycle of Fasting, the Cycle of the Continuum Sacrament, the Cycle of Mantramic Speaking and the Cycle of Tithing fulfills Cyclic Law. Thus, one takes his destiny in his own hands, self-willing, self-creating. This is the Self-Genesis Gift: Self-Creation.

Every cycle has a rhythm and intelligence. By using knowledge of the cycles, one develops intuition beyond ordinary instinctual nature. Instinctual nature relates to the reflex energy-laws. Cyclic intuition provides one with prophetic and seership insights, whereby seeming miracles occur. If one responds to cycles, he immediately moves into the Coinciding Principle.

Every time one has a rise of aware-joy, he should move with it; this is the beginning of a Cycle. He should keep the energy of joy alive through the Divine Pleasure-Principle of Bliss, and he will reap the rewards of happiness, peace.

Cycles are Ultimates set as Eternal Cause. If one fails to fulfill with full virtue the energy in a cycle, he will inevitably be exposed to the lower aspect of a cycle which will contain the unmanifested and misused energies of the cycle he neglected or ignored.

Cycles are mechanized into one's life as destiny. When one fails to move with the momentum of a cycle, he must retrieve his knowing and learning; through experiencing, he harmoniously unites with the intention of the cycle. Every cycle has its own intelligible, and concludes itself inevitably as intelligence.

A cycle can go by one; this may be likened to missing a train. To understand Cyclic Law is to go with the momentum of the Law. Every cycle goes where it is supposed to go, accomplishing the Law of God. Cycles are part of the Law-process supporting the equilibrium system of all worlds, all earths.

Through grace, a cycle comes like an express train, providing the comforts of swift, attractive and safe travel to one's destination. If one responds and flows with the cycle, he has used his grace. However, if one, by tamas nature or rajasic ego, refuses to respond and move with his cycle, he is like a person who must take a local train rather than an express. His units of measure are karmic rather than grace; his travel is painful, blundering, awkward and unknowing.

Man should learn never to be surprised or disappointed, but should welcome that which gives a death knell to his fixity, to his resisting, to his own desire to be in the shallow waters of life rather than the immersion within the Cosmos.

Jesus understood Cycles and Timing. He understood duration. He understood units of measure.

TIMING AND THE HOLY CYCLES

The Good Cycles prepare one for the Holy Cycles.

One gains access to the Holy and Superior Cycles through grace. Grace selects the timing to place its diamond-energy into the timing of the Coinciding Cycles through which men exceed the physical and enter into the spiritual.

The disciple must be at all times aware when he has been presented with a creative and illuminative cycle. Such cycles stem from spiritual accumulative grace of the ages. These cycles bring with them a unique anointing for placement and recognition of holy powers.

When a Saint's time has come, his cycle draws him up into the Holy Omnipresence where he is accompanied by the Angels, the Saints, and all of the providence in fellowship necessary to impregnate his mission into the souls of men in the world.

Before one can earn the *Holy Cycles*, he must have manifested in the Maya functioning the *Good Cycles*. These Good Cycles exist as blessing stages through which one is approved by the mass or selected for some unique fulfillment through which the masses are benefited.

One is in the *Good Cyclic Timing* because he has fulfilled the virtue of character and trust, the virtue of humaneness and compassion, the virtue of honesty and integrity, the virtue of right relationships in attitude toward race, nation and religion.

In the latter days of Self-Genesis, there will be many more men in the Earth who have inherited the Good Cycles through their own virtue-stamina. The world is a pleasanter place for those who know, or are acquainted with, or exposed to, any one having reached the Good Cyclic Timing through virtue and grace. In the latter part of Self-Genesis, there will be many more of these good ones in the world. Such ones will be preparing for the Holy Cyclic Timing in their life and soul expression.

In this time of homogeneity between lower Self-Genesis and higher Self-Genesis, those who lean toward God are being prepared to enter the Good Cycles, that men of the Earth may be calmed, cured, and made hopeful in their vision for the future.

Proving all things through good as being healing for all is a true religiosity. A true religiosity prepares those who think and live through religiosity-intuition for service to God. When one turns toward service for God first in all things, he has entered into Good Cyclic Timing.

THE MATHEMATICS OF THE CYCLES OF THE ARCHETYPES

We are now heirs to the Greater Archetypes facing a new human-race cycle.

The Mathematics of the Cycles enable one to understand the lesser and the greater Archetypal Days. There are periodic impulses which determine the Genesis states of man in his evolutionary processes. The Mathematics of Cycles lead man directly to Universal Mathematics whereby he unites with rhythmic compulsions directly sent forth from God as Spirit.

The rhythmic impulses relate to the Greater-Archetypal Days; the cyclic impulses, to the Moving-Archetypal Days. The Greater-Archetypal Days occur every 250,000 years. The Moving-Archetypal Cyclic Days occur every 12,000 years.

Four Genesis-Cycles in a Moving Archetype repeat themselves in each Moving-Archetypal Cycle, always seeking to become more refined and sensitized. Each Moving Archetype has four *Yugas* or Ages.

At the end of a 10,000-year period in a Moving Archetype, there is a 2,000-year level of God-knowing. God-knowing, regardless of the level of knowing in a person, relates to three things: (1) knowing of existence, (2) knowing of knowledge, and (3) knowing of God. In a 2,000-year Archetypal-Interim period, those who are less evolved will know God only as existence, as life. Those who are Niscient or *Knowing* will know God directly through Soul-experience. Those who know God as Bliss, will achieve Samadhi, and will be of those 144,000 who will enter the Saviour Path or Bodhisattva Path to assist all others in the world to achieve God-knowing.

In every 12,000-year Moving Archetype, during the 2,000-year Interim time those who are ready to enter into the true Bodhisattva enlightenment become the spiritual avatars for the next Moving Archetype.

SOUL-RHYTHM CYCLES

The recognition of the Cycles in one's life is connected with Self-Realization and Soul-Realization— and that is when one takes command of the Cyclic Law.

Everything one does activates a Cycle or a correspondence to Cyclic Law. Every Cycle is as a seed carrying its own Archetypal compulsion to expand. If it is a negative cycle or seed, one must undergo the full processes of the negative in the cyclic distribution through cause and effect. Therefore, it is important in the spiritual life to understand Cyclic Law as a part of Karmic Law. The one way this can be understood and consciously regulated is through the practice of Marking and Tracing.

When one knows his origin, he can prophesy his ending. Through Marking and Tracing, one learns to make right choices, to relax his rigidities fixed upon possessivism. All must give space or room for the debris falling away from claims and ambitions. If one stands in the way of his own fall-out of negation, he courts disaster.

All Cycles have many varying circulatory laps. To receive the grace to unite with a *master lap* in a Cycle *is* grace. Each lap in a Cycle contains a degree or unit of measure which defines and determines for the one moving into the Cycle how it can be utilized or not utilized.

There are fluent laps in a Cycle and electrically over-charged laps in a Cycle. There are benign laps in a Cycle. These are experienced on the level of the cyclic automation which has been set up with the creation of a solar or eternity system.

Cycles are unavoidable, for they are a part of progressing and increasing within the Will of God. If one misreads his cyclic opportunity as offered by the soul, he becomes a school-learner without promise of promotion.

When the true Cyclic Rhythm appears — and the chela or disciple is unready to move with the Cycle — the Cyclic pattern is depressed into a less spiritualized Cycle. During such times, a chela often becomes very depressed, experiencing a little spiritual death, or a cycle of dryness.

When one seeks to enter into the soul-flow of Rhythmic Cycles loaded with the baggage of karmas which he is unwilling to resolve, the weight of the karma automatically slows down the cyclic energy as offered in the Soul Cycle.

The major times of a Soul Cycle in the life of each person are the 35th year, the 42nd year, the 49th year and the 56th year. If one is unaware of the Soul Rhythms, he is faced with the heavier restitution-demands of his karma.

If a person in his 35th year refuses to turn to God, he has lost touch with his religiosity-grace, and thereafter must flounder in the agnosticism of non-belief.

If one in the 42nd year has ignored his Soul Rhythm, he is as a child six years old still seeking to be nursed and, especially, indulged through the Feminine Principle.

When one who reaches the 49th year has thwarted or ignored the rhythmic, cyclic flow of the Soul, he returns to puberty and adolescence values and morality. He seeks to individualize singularly his passions. He deserts marital and work functional obligations, asserting the right to do his own thing.

In the 56th year, if one has listened to and responded to the Soul-Rhythm cyclic periods, he may be likened to a man who can look back upon his life's events as victory, giving to him in this time the compounded interest of his virtue. In such virtue reaping of grace-wisdom, he makes a covenant to plan the future of his years as service to God.

If one reaches the year of 56, having ignored the three previous Cycles, he will find himself unsupported by the vigor of his former etheric impulses. His health and his psychological state will have shattered as to his reasoning regarding success or failure, happiness or love. In the 56th year, the lower etheric body absent from the Soul-Rhythm Cycles begins a death process for both the physical and lower etheric bodies.

One who has failed to observe the Soul Rhythms is living in a self-destruct body no longer energized to health or vital joy. Thereafter, it is inevitable for him to lean toward death in thought and action.

And he began to teach them that the Son of man must suffer many things, and be rejected of the elders, and of the chief priests, and scribes, and be killed, and after three days rise again.

—*St. Mark 8:31*

It is the law existing in the Soul-Rhythm Cycles that one who believes he is deathless, and that consciousness lives on after death, experiences after the last heartbeat of the physical body three days of introspection or roll-back of his karma and the meaning of the life just relinquished. This is experienced in three ways: Tamas, Rajas and Sattvic. During the first three days after death, the first day is Tamas; the second day, Rajas; the third day, Sattvic.

The first day after death is a *red* day. The second day is a *yellow* day. The third day is a *white* day. On the red day, one separates himself from his physical hold on the Earth. On the yellow day, he releases himself to the etheric knowledge of his true nature and everlasting body. On the white or third day, one enters into Heaven, and finds himself in his soul-home.

On the first or red day, one must encounter purgatory with the help of the Jesus Mediation, wherein he sees the suffering of unredeemed souls. On the second or yellow day, he enters into the grace-planes of life, and sees all souls as one.

On his second day, one accepts how his karma can be balanced for his next life on Earth. If his debts are heavy, he will go into a sleep until his next birth on Earth. If his grace is present, he will be shown how he can serve in Heaven to lift souls seeking God and to relieve man's ignorance of God, and heal the fallen souls who can learn of God through the Angels.

On the third or white day, one becomes one with his Angels, with his Grace, and with God as the One. On this third day, he accepts where and how he can serve in Heaven.

A child forms in the womb in a nine-month cycle. This Soul-Rhythm Cycle is divided into three three-month cycles. The first three months are Tamas; genetic incubation. The second three months are Rajas. The third three months are Sattvic; preparation for thrust into the world.

> *The etheric body is the body of Time and Space and Cycles.*

FATE AND DESTINY CYCLES THROUGH NUMBERS

> *. . . the very hairs of your head are all numbered.*
> —*St. Matthew 10:30*

The 0 numbers, such as 60, 70 or 80 years of age, are vitally important in research of Earth-purpose or life in Earth.

The double numbers, such as 33, 44, 55, 66 are important in the assaying of the units of measure as to the use of time.

In the double numbers, one may encounter death as the end, as did Jesus in His 33rd year. However, death contains resurrection. If used with acceptable reverence, the 33rd, 44th, 55th and 66th years can resurrect a total life on the level of the soul, on the level of the mind, on the level of love, on the level of the physical and etheric.

These years as units of measure are cycles of fate and destiny. One has choice as to how he uses the component quality and quantity in the energy of these double-numbered years.

The same refers also to an 11th day, 22nd day and a 33rd day. These are resurrection times for the soul to shine forth from behind its cloud of karmas in the soul-record.

These cyclic, double-numbered days are both fate and destiny. One stands in the units of measure as one who collects both energy and essence or the Esse of the Holy Spirit.

The cycles of destiny work with the Rhythm of the Eternals, of the Cosmos. The cycles of fate work with predestined, cyclic, energized after-effects. Man learns first through after-effects rather than cause. In uniting with destiny or rhythmic cycles, he unites with Cause. Anyone having the grace to live within the rhythms of destiny knows the Cause and commands his fate.

OLD SOULS AND YOUNG SOULS: RHYTHMS OF REINCARNATION

I will have another day.
I will have a spring.
I will have another sunset.
And I will have another sun.

I will fan the fire.
I will flail the wind.
I will reap the fruits.
And I will plant the seed again.

I will make a roar.
I will learn to swim.
I will dance the breath
When I am born again.

An Old Soul has the power to select his timing to return to the world. He has the awareness of *why* he comes and he knows where he is going; and he knows the reason for his coming to the world through birth.

An Old Soul reincarnates more rapidly than a Young Soul. Having earned grace in this eternity system or some other, he reincarnates more frequently and is thus termed an *Old Soul*. A *Young Soul* is one who has come from a former eternity system having less acceleration. Such souls are dependent upon the reincarnation tidal-waves to bring them to birth.

An Old Soul works with the pure Sattvic light. A Young Soul works with the tamasic; and in the present era, with the rajasic.

The True Self determines how the soul is used. The True Self, through the state of God-awareness, uses the Soul-Power to reincarnate by choice in an environment, place, family or nation. The karma and the unknowing of a Young Soul determine his placement, his family, his nation, his religion, his race.

There are *interim* incarnations and there are *vital* incarnations.

During a Kali-Yuga time, persons who remember past lives and know reincarnation as a reality have the responsibility of passing on the truths of karma and reincarnation. Among those who are the foremost supporters keeping alive truths are the Masters and the Master Teachers.

All who are living within the knowledge of reincarnation and applying this principle are advanced souls — probationers of the Universal. Such souls as *Teachers* recognize the necessity to fulfill the Law. They base their teachings upon the fulfilling of the Law.

Among these probationers are some less-advanced as souls. They intuit the truth in the Law of Reincarnation, yet have not the full command of the rhythm within this Law. Such persons have speeded up their incarnation-rhythms but have yet to earn choice in their polarities as to birth. These are the chelas of Old Souls or students who hunger after life everlasting; however, by some inertia in their birth natures, they are the mid-gap ones who know, but do not apply that which they know.

Death is a rest between reincarnations. Some souls, by their evils, are drawn into the "outer darkness" spoken of by Jesus. These are in the state of darkness or *refrigeration*. There are other souls who are in the twilight zone who must await the tidal wave of a propitious massive-reincarnation; these are in *incubation*. Then there are souls who are energized through awareness of God who are free to reincarnate. Those who are less articulate as to God reincarnate more slowly.

Souls who are free in the Logos Spirit of God reincarnate by choice, placing themselves where their time on Earth will be utilized to the uttermost for the good of God and man.

If one experiences a *dry birth* on the reincarnation scale, his soul has sent him back into the world to suffer internally. He is in a prolonged banishment state in the physical world. He will have periodic spells of agony and of a remorse he is unable to identify. He looks out of his eyes with black agony, for his soul is mirroring the torment of his own ecclesiastical evils of the past.

If one is on the ego-level, he judges everything through the external and personal.

The Great Privilege given of God is that He gave men the privilege to co-create as co-creators with Him. However, the price for this privilege is that in each life one must re-earn this privilege.

Privileged environments and authorities are given to one through past earning. In each life and situation within a life, one must re-earn that which he has earned in previous lives. He must prove in every single act that he is worthy of the stewardship of privilege. If he has failed to understand privilege as being divine, he becomes bankrupt. Through selfishness and self-exaltation, one can obliterate *privileged-grace*.

The Maya system is a system of work, sweat, tears, suffering. In each life, one must seek happiness through the channels of divine being. Happiness and contentment in the Maya world are impossible without awareness of God and of His Grace.

The Maya system does not tolerate anyone who takes too

much or anyone who gives too little. Pain comes when one has taken too much; and when one has given too little, Maya demands restitution—for service to God must be *more* before one can satisfy the balancing-energies of Maya.

Maya has the rules, and God has the Laws. If one lives wholly within the rules of Maya, he lives a God-life or Sattva life without difficulty.

Luck is grace earned in past lives through the mastery of gravity.

WORK AND LAW: CYCLES OF PROSPERING

Beloved, I wish above all things that thou mayest prosper and be in health, even as thy soul prospereth.

—3 John 2

Work sets up its own cycle, and maintains its cyclic rhythm through dedication. Work as a self-responsible function is the beginning of creation, whereby man masters the unruly forces of his psychism, and enters into discrimination and intuition.

Before Jesus, men thought in their collective instincts. Through Jesus, men are more individualized. It is the design for men through Jesus to become self-responsible. Only through work and creation is this possible.

It is God's pleasure to give to man His Kingdom. In the Kingdom of God each man has his own domain. The domain or place of craftsmanship is determined by the gyroscope of the soul.

"The desire of the slothful killeth him; for his hands refuse to labour." (Proverbs 21:25) He who is an outcast of society has refused at some time to work in the spirit of service, and can only return to human-spirit and soul vocation through work as a service to God.

When man is self-controlled, the spirit of his ancestors rejoices in Heaven. When man is self-reliant, his ego is anointed with soul-faculties. When man is self-responsible, he is given a domain to rule, wherein he honors God and all kingdoms, domains.

God gives the opportunity to anyone who is willing to work. If one is too lazy to work, he will never be united with God.

A mystic who works has a chance. A mystic who refuses to work has no chance.

The Teacher loves people who "pitch in."

Work and law are twins; they are simultaneous; they work together. Without willingness to work as service to God and the human race, man suffers under law, and is unpaid for his efforts. Success minus the law is ephemeral, unreal and non-lasting.

The soul adores the sound of the Law because the soul desires to escape from the unlawful. Great-Soul-line Teachers teach to the soul. The hearing soul through the Law responds to the Law speaking through his Teacher.

The first Law for the soul-freedom is the Law of giving and receiving. To receive the Law and to exemplify it is Liberation.

The Absolute Inevitables of Law are:

> *If one hates work, he will end up being a servant.*
> *If one loves money more than he loves God, he*
> *will end up in poverty.*
> *If one loves things of lust, he will end up with*
> *disease.*

Character is the outer evidence of the inner responding to Law for many lives. To be born with character testifies to pure, selfless will throughout many existences. The essential sign of character is courage.

The first indication of a person's character is his attitude toward work. Work is salvation's key to Self-Realization.

Jesus changed the burden in work to the yoke of creation. Man finds his work through the barometer of his stomach. Man finds his creation through the gyroscope of his soul.

Work must come first. The discipline of work produces character. Character produces ethic. Ethic provides the vehicle for conscience and consciousness, whereby one maintains all vehicles.

The only thing that will cleanse out the aftermath of repentance—which is remorse—is the fire of work. Work is fire, and there is nothing more cleansing than work for God. When work is absent from thoughts of recognition or rewards, given totally as a service to God, one is free from his sins, and his remorse has become a blessing-vehicle for the world and for God.

Life is a banking system. Man must continually work as a steward to build up his repository of grace, in that he might make more grace and reap the dividends of grace by spending it to make grace.

God spends His dividends on man. Men are His heirs. They must use their inheritance and substance as stewards, as careful watchmen over their resources. If one has misspent his substance or has failed to earn it, he must re-earn his substance to become a responsible banker in the economics of energy.

> *Owe no man anything, but to love one another:*
> *for he that loveth another hath fulfilled the law.*
> *—Romans 13:8*

"*Owe no man . . .*" If one borrows money from a person, he is connected with him karmically. "*The rich ruleth over the poor, and the borrower is servant to the lender.*" (*Proverbs 22:7*)

A worker and a shirker are usually together in the lower aspects of marriage. When marriage is no longer bondage, then workers unite—and the perfect marriage brings the chaste stewardship; for where two work as one, the Will of God has begun for the human race. Work mates, when in harmony with the creativity flow in the opposite mate, eventually earn the right to produce for God a conjoined work or co-atom channeling in service to God.

> *Labour not for the meat which perisheth, but for that meat which endureth unto everlasting life, which the Son of man shall give unto you: for him hath God the Father sealed.*
> —St. John 6:27

HOLY HAVING

> *Whereof I was made a minister, according to the gift of the grace of God given unto me by the effectual working of his power. Unto me, who am less than the least of all saints, is this grace given, that I should preach among the Gentiles the unsearchable riches of Christ.*
> —Ephesians 3:7,8

Money is like everything else—it must be used with reverence. Money is as dangerous as a murderer's knife when it is used wrongly.

More souls have been lost in the markets of money than in any other process of life. Therefore, in getting money, one should get honor, integrity, gratitude, reverence and Agape or a giving spirit, that the Holy Spirit may use his Soul Temple as a Temple for God in which the Altar is upright and sacred. And he who goes in to this Altar shall be fed, replenished, and made whole.

Holy Impoverishment comes to him who uses the Altar of God as a market place. It is grace of first order when one who has strayed from right stewardship experiences Holy Impoverishment.

As Job must undergo a time-interval to return to his Holy Having, so must each person who declares the Name of God and uses His gold to earn his Holy Having, that he might serve the many.

When Nature is violated extravagantly, Prakriti as Nature destroys. Extravagance produces abnormality in balance.

Whenever one meets a need and answers a need, it is legitimate in Heaven and on Earth. This is the only lawful prospering. This is then the Grace of Holy Having, for God needs those who revere His Increase and use it to serve devotion. Holy Having and Holy Prospering work with the virtue of the winged Angels.

He who uses Mammon as his god is serving but one — that is, the ego-self. However, he who takes on the burdens of the impoverishment of the many, and would open the riches of the Christ, must be God-centered, balanced, modest. He who serves the Altar of God to unveil His riches must understand the Spirit of God within His abundance.

The shepherd of the sheep leads the sheep to the pasture where all is green, where still waters are nigh. If a shepherd chooses the pasture for his own glamorization, the grass dies at the root; the sheep starve.

God supports His Universe — financial, physical, emotional and mental — through an economy which is set to Eternal Law. Man seeking to invent eternity laws to control the Economy of God is fated to bankruptcy.

Everything can be resolved when the Economic Laws of God are fulfilled to the last jot and tittle. He who serves in the small with a whole heart is given enlightenment and enlargement within the Holy Having and Increase of God.

THE TITHING CYCLE AND THE INCREASE OF GOD

Bring ye all the tithes into the store house, that there may be meat in mine house, and prove me

now herewith, saith the Lord of hosts, if I will not
open you the windows of heaven, and pour you out
a blessing, that there shall not be room enough to
receive it.

—Malachi 3:10

There are preordained cycles that take hold of a man's life. These keep him united with Cosmos, with God. The preordained cycles are spiritualized cycles. They compel man to remain united with the Constant of God in him.

There are man-made cycles which are ruled and controlled by self-cycle manipulation through the lower mind as desire. The lower cycles are karmic cycles which must be mastered by the ordained cycles.

Man makes his ego-fate through the lower side of his cyclic nature. He builds his grace through the ordained cycles. In initiatory victories and Illumination, he takes hold of the lower-cyclic compulsions and opens himself fully to God-Realization.

In the Scriptures, the initiatory story of Cain and Abel relates to Cain who worked with lower cyclic law or self-claiming, fatalism. Abel represented ordained cyclic law; his tithe was accepted because he understood God and Cosmos as related to the soul of man. Abel gave the soul-gifts; Cain gave the body-gifts. These two prototypes exist throughout the Earth: one who takes and one who gives.

The tithe offered by Cain and Abel, Esau and Jacob, and Judas and Jesus concerns all who live in the Earth. Abel and Jacob and Jesus represent those who follow the etheric laws. Abel gave through his soul-gifts to God. So did Jacob. So did Jesus. In the etheric laws, everything belongs to God. When man gives his portion of substance to God as an offering, he is returning it to God for God to multiply, and it will be restored to him bountifully. God returns the giving of the offering "pressed down and running over" (St. Luke 6:38) to one who gives the gifts of his soul to God, the One.

The offering of Cain benefited through limitation or the perishable because it was given with the idea that it would nourish only the physical. The soul-gifts given by Abel were taken by the Father and seeded and planted into the Heavenly Gardens of Substance which are infinite and unlimited.

He who gives a tithe in the spirit of Cain is feeding limitation in Maya. He who gives a tithe in the spirit of Abel is fed forever; he and his kind are fed forever.

The two priceless things one cannot buy are *Faith* and *Love*. One cannot buy the Word of God, but one can, through a true strength and vital gift of the self and of faith, be ever in the Presence of God, receiving His bountifulness, His guidance, His protection.

One cannot have what he has not, nor be what he is not. The bread or the gift of life offered through the Word of God on His Holy Altar becomes a stone when one seeks to buy the Truth or the life within the Holy Spirit. God cannot be purchased, neither can He be coerced through monies, possessions or objects.

True propitiation, supplication and prayer with the most choice and precious offering — the self for God — are acceptable on His Altar. All that one has has been given of God. By giving what one is, one fulfills the Image of God within. All energies turned toward God with selflessness in heart and mind empower the Presence of God within to act as Love, as Light, as Life, as Will.

Altars built upon enforced doctrine and creed are absent from the Word of God; such altars preserve ideals built upon separateness called creeds. Creedless worship, faithful hearts, devotee application and attendance of the Holy Spirit within the Scriptures keep alive the offerings, the faith, the devotion, the worship upon the Holy Altar of God.

There is but one Altar of God. This is the Altar in the heart. When the mind wills as an ego, the Altar of God in the

heart is as cold ashes snuffed out by the little will. The heart
furnishes the fuel for the mind. If the heart be without love,
there is no fire or light in the mind.

It is inevitable that the heart's desire for love begins with
the fires of suffering. The bright sparkle of the mind ignited
in the Holy Spirit begins always with the first coal of fire ignited in the Altar of the heart.

A tithe to support the Word of God supports the life within
the Word. The selfless dedication through and with the tithe
spiritualizes and transenergizes the gross flame of life into the
pure flame of life. With each tithe, the virtues of life coming from the Word bless the many in the world.

He who fears to tithe in the spirit of supporting the Word
of God starves his body of grace. The Word of God is instant,
quick. In supporting the Word of God through tithing, one
retrieves his spirituality and enters into the plentitude-
blessings abiding in every living thing.

A barren heart produces barren gifts and giving. A barren mind produces ignorance, limitation. An empty hand
denotes an empty heart. To walk in the Path of Truth, one
must be full in heart, open in mind to what God saith to him
within the Altar of the heart.

Tithing as an act to still the conscience bears little fruit;
yet, one gesture from the prompting of conscience assists in
preserving the Word of God. When one moves beyond
conscience-giving as rectification for sin, and gives with his
holy nature, he becomes whole within the Omnipresence of
God. He becomes magnanimous.

A knower of Creation is a giver. He does not give so that
he may receive for his giving. There is a mystery in giving to
support the Word of God; this mystery is that one becomes
Godly, and thereby is anointed within the Power of God.

When one does not have, God is taking away from him
because he misused what He gave. The first tithe given as a
support of the Word of God and its spreading is as a small

stone, a pebble containing a hidden jewel which becomes the bread or the manna of life supporting the crucial needs over the cruel lack in the world. The stone of poverty is verily turned into bread when the spirit of giving within the tithing is given to the Altar of God.

Reluctance to tithe impoverishes. In tithing, one receives the whole. In impoverished giving, one receives but a portion of the loaf.

A person who desires to take back his gift given to support the Word of God invites future impoverishment spiritually and materially. One who seeks to commercialize his gift to the Altar becomes a victim of financial manipulation. Religions devoid of tithe-responsibility become materialistic, begging institutions.

Sacred is the Law of Tithing. He who keeps it comes into the First Covenant: God is Omnipotent in spiritual and human affairs. To take one of the Laws of God and put it in one's life is to untie the tangled knots in everything and to place them back into rightness.

We give 10% to God and He gives 90% back to us. It is overwhelming to realize how generous God is to give us 90% of His Creation while we give or offer to Him our meager 10% of creation.

One's tithes spread the Word of God as a service to God. In giving his tithe, one must *believe* that his tithe is expendable as good for those who would hear and benefit from the Word.

All feel they are ineffectual in explaining and describing God. God has given to us the Law of the Tithe as compensation for our inadequacy in describing Him. The tithe is therefore first a support for a rightful way of describing God; of making God known; and of making God present to those who have need of knowing and living God. Secondly, the tithe blesses one's own personal prospering, assuring him of the

Providence of a caring Father who knows his need. Thirdly, to tithe, one budgets his source of income within the Increase of God, whereby his offering to God as a tithe stimulates the opportunity for advancement in the physical world.

In budgeting under the blessing of giving a tithe, one becomes a steward of energies represented by monies, houses, lands, objects and the needful exercise in going and coming as related to God's service. When one tithes, he is placing his mundane powers in trust to the Holy Spirit, whereby the compounded dividends return to him as prospering in all bodies and expressions of self.

The Increase of God holds the key through the tithe.

> *The tenth shall be holy unto the Lord.*
> —*Leviticus 27:32*

THE THREE ENERGY FORCES

The three force voltages of *Tamas, Rajas* and *Sattva* — the three Gunas — follow through the total Creation. To focus one's mind upon these three is to unravel the Universe and to unravel one's own life as a person and as a being. The most excellent way of gaining insights into the benefits of Marking and Tracing is through the understanding of the three processes of energy sustaining Creation.

The Gunas are in control of the exchange between Cycles — that is, the crossing over is determined by the three force voltages within the Cycles:

1. The cycle man makes in his habit patterns;

2. The cycle man must meet in his karma through Initiation;

3. And the cycle which is the God-Realized instrument for Illumination.

Units of measure in consciousness depend upon one's knowledge of the three force voltages. Eternal attributes flow within these three. One therefore must understand this positive Law upholding all Creation: the Father, the Son, the Holy Spirit; the Tamas, the Rajas, the Sattvic.

God as the Eternal Presence in Creation or the Holy Spirit in the Atma begins His functioning with the Sattvic; following is the Rajasic; then, through density, His Spirit becomes the Tamasic. Man, using the building aspect of Creation, begins with Tamas; energizes and particularizes into the Rajasic; transcends in the Sattvic, and masters with mind the versatilities of God.

If it were not for Holy Spirit within Tamas, there would be no consciousness or awareness. If the Son were absent from the Rajasic, there would be no direct consciousness or the power to discover through the processes of the individual mind. If the Father were absent from the Sattvic, there would be no spiritual involvement; soul would be absent and empty; the Constant would fail to reproduce God as Will, Life, Light, Love.

THE GUNA SYSTEM OF TIME AND CYCLES

The Guna rhythms are experienced in three-day cycles throughout the year. One may find the clue to the energy-flows of his days by his understanding of the three Gunas.

Each Guna functions through an aspect of God: Ganesha (Tamas); Hanuman (Rajas); and Garuda (Sattva).

The symbol of the Elephant pertains to Ganesha. Ganesha is the unheard thunder. A Ganesha Day is a Tamasic Day. The mystery of the order of the Universe is concealed in Tamasic fixities and rigidities. On the negative side in consciousness, this occurs as resistance, unused power, inertia.

Ganesha relates to will power and also to the atomic energy

at the end of the spine, or the first station of Kundalini. The elephant as a symbol represents the largest inert-mass transportation creature. As a day of inert matter, a Ganesha Day expresses tamas, or man's unknowing of the vast accumulated energies in his own nature.

Ganesha contains the latent power as energy to be exploded through movement and motion. The mind on a Ganesha Day, using the tamas energy, transenergizing it into motion, produces explosions of power through consciousness.

A Ganesha Day presents to each disciple a challenge in the use of power. Ganesha represents the ethic of keeping promises, and thereby freeing oneself from limit in time, restriction in action. Ignoring a Ganesha energy potential produces lethargy, atrophy and death. Utilizing the latent inertia of the tamas as symbolized by Ganesha, one takes a leap into greater utilization of consciousness.

The symbol of the monkey relates to Hanuman. A Hanuman Day is a Rajasic Day. Rajas energy, when scattered, is excitable will-power.

A Hanuman Day, the Day of the Monkey, represents incessant movement, restlessness of the mind, and involvement in lesser Self-Genesis and Human-Genesis affairs. Personalized contacts on a rajasic day, communications; all relate to surface issues until one learns to extend the Hanuman power of mastery over duality. A Rajasic Day is an extremely good day for Marking and Tracing of one's personal motive.

The symbol of Garuda relates to man as half-bird and half-man. As a bird, he is free to fly or enter into other realms; as man, he is gravity-bound to the Earth. A Garuda Day is a Sattvic Day. Garuda represents polarity energies between man as a soaring spirit and as a walker on the path of life.

The Garuda power of the bird-man gives the power to have out-of-body vision, extended night-flight, third-wisdom consciousness. A sattvic day can produce peace, inspiration, insight with a vision beyond the physical.

When Sattva falls on a Saturday, it is a Hierarchy Day; a Day of the Archangels and the Great Devas; a day of Buddhi and the revealing within the Buddhi or the Informing Principle.

Every initiate who has a spiritual experience should ask himself: "What day is it? Is it a Tamasic, Rajasic or Sattvic Day?" By the Guna, he will know what his vision is, and what his work is for the day. He will also recognize his cycle, and learn how to accept the grace or karma it brings.

On a Tamas Day, one should be thorough, plodding, methodical. He should observe his senses; he should prove all things as to his sense of taste, touch, sight, sound and smell.

A Rajasic Day is a Service Day, whereby one overcomes the tumults of the tamasic and the rajasic. On a Rajasic Day, one should extend his senses through the power of the will. Through conscious self-control and self-responsibility, he should seek to stabilize the electrifying rapidity of his magnification as to power, force, willing. He should seek to do unto others as he would have them do unto him. On a Rajasic Day, he is a maker in charge of his own creation, good or ill.

On a Sattvic Day, one should lean upon the column strength of love, harmlessness, peace and mediation. He should take advantage of the Sattvic-nature of unlimited purities, of mediative states of happiness and bliss.

One begins to think with energy self-discerning thoughts when he thinks through the Gunas. Every tamasic Guna has within it a concealed rajasic and concealed sattvic. The initiate masters the tamas energy through drawing forth the rajasic as stability and taking hold of the sattvic as his birthright-portion of Earth. Every Tamas Day contains periods of uncontrolled rajas and of mystical flashing-points of sattvic spirituality.

In all things related to the exploring and discovering processes of the soul, one must take hold of the most apparent and obvious. All Tamas Days are strong and powerful days promising certain aspects of power. The tamas relates to the Unmanifest. On a Tamasic Day, one can delve into the potentials of power. On a Rajasic Day, one can see how to use this awesome aspect of force and energy. How he uses it determines what the Unmanifest will do outwardly for him.

On a Sattvic Day, if one has any remaining tamas in his nature, the desire for peace may mesmerize him to slothful regression, and make the sattvic into the tamas, rather than the true Ahimsa of Peace.

To think and act with cognizance within the Gunas is to see truly the wondrous design and scope within the proclivities for life. To make chaste the Guna-cycles and the days, one should resolve to be ever perceptive. The most-high aspect of the Divine Mind in man represents quality and purity within the mental aspect of reasoning.

Countless tone-sounds accompany the Tamas, slow and somber. Billions and billions of staccatos of interrelated tones affecting the soul-waves in consciousness relate to the Rajasic. The mighty Sattvic soul-wave of music entering life as music transcendent transports the Initiate into dimensional realms of knowing God and of God-Realization.

The cruel face of Maya appears to all who must struggle for life in Maya Earth-existence. In the Gunas, all is maintained, balanced, ever-changing, never still, never quiet. This symphony of the Gunas contains the energy of the Spirit of God, whereby He is ever in the state of Increase and Creation.

Tamas-tears shed are tears of futility. Bitterness against God as Creator is overcome when one knows that not one Guna can work singly as all or completeness, but that these three play within and upon each other to uphold the becoming man as divine, as true within the Plan and Will of God.

It is rajasic and self-deceitful when man through unusual invention thinks he has taken charge of life and of life-processes. Everything created by man is dependent upon the play of the three Gunas. Were it not for the interplay of the energies within the Gunas, there would be no stuff of life. The Earth is an existing orbit through which the three aspects of God creating as the Gunas energize man toward Hierarchy fulfillment.

The extravagent use of Time is a Rajasic and Tamasic trait. One must balance the Time-units and understand the Guna Cyclic Law to gain the full rewards in the use of Time.

Who can truly say to himself on the taking of a piece of bread: "How long did it take for this wheat-seed to be planted or for the harvest and utilization in the making and the baking of the bread?" How often does man discern the bread in its taste, in its nourishment, from the seed to the blood to the mind?

Every particle of energy contains the three Gunas. Only through reverence for God, for His Will, His Life, His Light and His Love can one truly understand the gift of Time-energy in the taking of a morsel of bread. Someone's planting, someone's reaping, someone's offering, have placed this bread in his hand, in his body. Guna nourishment and Guna balance are obtained in only one way: Reverence for God, for Life, for Self, for All.

The dance of the Gunas brings all to the world, takes all from the world. In this unending dance, there is no death, only birth.

Jesus, who understood the timing in the planting of the seed, and finally of the bread, was able to give the fishes and the loaves to the thousands. He understood the Guna Cycles. He was a Master of Time and Space as experienced in the world of Creation through mind, body and soul.

GRACE

The Lord God is a sun and shield: the Lord will give grace and glory: no good thing will he withhold from them that walk uprightly.

—Psalm 45:2

God is able to make all grace abound toward you; that ye, always having all sufficiency in all things, may abound to every good work.

—St. Paul, *2 Corinthians 9:8*

God resisteth the proud, but giveth grace unto the humble.

—James 4:6

Wherefore gird up the loins of your mind, be sober, and hope to the end for the grace that is to be brought unto you at the revelation of Jesus Christ.

—1 Peter 1:13

It is for God to grant His grace. Your task is to accept that grace and guard it.

—St. Cyril of Jerusalem (died 386)

It is not in virtue of its liberty that the human will attains to grace, it is much rather by grace that it attains to liberty.

—St. Augustine, 425

The grace of Christ clothes us, as it were, with gorgeous purple and raises us to a dignity that surpasses all knowledge.

—St. Cyril of Alexandria (412–444)

Usually grace begins by illuminating the soul with a deep awareness, with its own light.

—Diodicus, 5th Century

The divinity is given us when grace penetrates our nature by a heavenly light, raising it above its natural condition by the greatness of glory.

—St. Maximus, c. 626

6

CYCLES OF INHERITANCE

God's Grace manifests in Cycles. Therefore,
O devotee, if you would come into a State of
Grace, learn of Cycles.

THE PRINCIPLE OF INHERITANCE

Remember me, O Lord, with the favour that
thou bearest unto thy people: O visit me with thy
salvation; That I may see the good of thy chosen,
that I may rejoice in the gladness of thy nation, that
I may glory with thine inheritance.
—Psalm 106:4,5

There are many inheritances to which each person is heir.
All levels and degrees of human life evolve and progress
through the Principle of Inheritance.

The DNA molecule, with its inheritances of memory,
enables mankind to maintain protective reflexes and intelligent reasoning, thereby preserving and prospering human
life as an integral part of the Creation of the Universe.

New stars in the Cosmos inherit certain energies from old
stars that die. Throughout Nature, the Principle of Inheritance is operative—from star to man, from tree to plant,
from animal to insect.

Each race, nation, religion and civilization inherits assets from former generations. These assets may be physical, spiritual, or both.

"Wisdom is good with an inheritance." *(Ecclesiastes 6:11)* From the religions of the world, mankind inherits the wisdom of the Saints, the Sages and other Enlightened Teachers. The knowledge of God, Holy Laws and Moral Principles is a priceless inheritance passed from one generation to another.

The Inheritance of the *Dharma,** the Inheritance of Scriptural instruction, the Inheritance of Grace from the Soul's Record of Past Lives, the Inheritance of National and Spiritual Freedoms — all are integral parts of the Principle of Inheritance.

The inheritance of monies, properties and possessions from family members or other loved ones who leave the world by death is a custom practiced in all cultures for all ages. One may also inherit from his ancestors and parents certain gene-traits, attitudes, talents.

"Houses and riches are the inheritance of fathers: and a prudent wife is from the Lord." *(Proverbs 19:14)* Through the Principle of Inheritance, a person may inherit from the Lord a healthy body, a loving and prudent mate, intelligent children. Every good thing in one's life is an inheritance from his forefathers, his soul's record, and from God.

"Moreover I call God for a record upon my soul." *(2 Corinthians 1:23)* The soul's record of each person is his inheritance from former lives. His present-life intelligence, skills, virtues and other blessings are among the many inheritances bequeathed to himself from past lives. Precious among the list of inheritances is the wisdom gained through countless lives of learning and experience recorded in the immortal record of the soul.

When one is a devoted and loyal servant of God and His

---

*Dharma is a Sanskrit word meaning truth, law, religion, virtue.

Son, he qualifies for spiritual inheritances beyond the inheritances of ancestors, parents, or the soul's record. All true servants of God are rewarded with imperishable inheritances that come only to the just, the righteous, the selfless.

> *And whatsoever ye do, do it heartily, as to the Lord, and not unto men; Knowing that of the Lord ye shall receive the reward of the inheritance: for ye serve the Lord Christ.*
> —*Colossians 3:23,24*

SPIRITUAL-BIRTHRIGHT INHERITANCE

> *Jesus said unto him, Thou shalt love the Lord thy God with all thy heart, and with all thy soul, and with all thy mind. This is the first and great commandment. And the second is like unto it, Thou shalt love thy neighbor as thyself.*
> —*St. Matthew 22:37–39*

In God's system of Inheritances, an earnest Truth-seeker receives numerous Inheritances of Grace. For one who fulfills the Commandments of Love, there are minor and major Inheritances of Grace received during the cyclic stages of his devotion to God.

As one progresses spiritually, his Grace-Inheritances increase profoundly; in this, he unites with the Providence of God, Who rewards the faithful, the righteous and the loving with the first fruits of His choicest blessings. To love God is to unite with His Bountifulness, His Magnanimity, His unceasing surprises of Grace and Truth.

Each minor and major Inheritance of Grace is preceded by a test of one's love for God and love for his fellow man. As long as one remains centered in the Commandments of Love, each Inheritance is received in its cyclic timing.

A *State of Grace* is a state of love-centering within the Expanding Grace of God. Thus, when one proves his love for God each day, and is selflessly dedicated to serving the human spirit, he is the recipient of expanding Grace-Inheritances. One Grace-Inheritance leads to the next Grace-Inheritance, thereby rewarding those who fulfill the Love-Commandments with ever-increasing measures of Grace.

Every test preceding a Grace-Inheritance relates to one's faith as well as his love. In every test, one or more virtues are thoroughly examined. If the Wisdom of God deems one worthy, a Grace-Inheritance is received by the aspirant in perfect timing. Should a Truth-seeker temporarily fail to qualify for a new Inheritance, the Inheritance will be received by him the moment he passes the test of his faith, love and virtue.

"Enter thou into the joy of thy lord." (St. Matthew 25:23) When one becomes aware of the fact that he is receiving many different kinds of Grace-Inheritances, he enters into the Joy of the Lord; he becomes an *heir* of the Living God—a son who has come of age spiritually.

A minor or major Cycle of Inheritance is never received out of timing. The Wisdom of God determines one's readiness or unreadiness. A true servant of God does not serve God with the thought of receiving from God; he thinks only of *giving* to God. This wholesome attitude and pure motive keeps one securely centered in the Love-Commandments through enlightened virtues and a clear conscience.

"God is not mocked: for whatsoever a man soweth, that shall he also reap." (Galatians 6:7) The greater the Inheritance of Grace, the greater is the test that precedes its receiving. God cannot be deceived, for He knows the thoughts of the heart and the mind, the motives, the intents; He knows the nature of one's love, the degree of each virtue. Through Grace-Inheritances, the Creator rewards His servants who ex-

press straightforwardness, honesty, honorableness, integrity, humility, and all other virtues. *"God . . . giveth grace unto the humble." (James 4:6)* The Grace that God gives to the humble is received through the wise and perfect Cycles of Inheritance.

> *The wise shall inherit glory: but shame shall be the promotion of fools.*
>
> *—Proverbs 3:35*

". . . Esau despised his birthright." (Genesis 25:34) Even as Esau despised his birthright, many persons despise their *Spiritual Birthright*. Every living soul, as a child of God, has a Spiritual Birthright; however, through the gift of free will, one may accept or reject his Spiritual Birthright. This is an individual decision.

The Spiritual-Birthright Inheritance is always available, for it is a Perpetual Gift from God. Enlightened Teachers tell about this Inheritance, and reveal the requirements for its attainment: the worship of God, works of righteousness, and selfless love.

The Spiritual-Birthright blessings are Image-of-God blessings. Into the Divine Image, God has sealed the seeds of every good and beautiful gift, reward, promise and inheritance. These seeds of sacred blessings manifest over the ages through one's Spiritual-Birthright Inheritance. To meditate upon the Image of God; to contemplate Eternal Life as a Cosmos Truth; to apply the teachings of Jesus; and to live according to the Commandments of God prepare one to receive his Spiritual Birthright.

The Spiritual Birthright of man is Eternal. As one increases his capacity to love and to understand, the Grace and Graciousness of God bless him with new ways to behold the splendor of His Universal Plan and the beauty of His Countenance: Absolute Truth.

At first, one holds forth a small, thimble-sized cup of faith for God to fill with His Spirit. As one grows in spiritual stature, he offers his heart and mind for God to fill with His Spirit. When one holds forth the Cosmos as a Cup for God to fill with His Spirit, he stands ready to claim the Greater Glories of his Spiritual-Birthright Inheritance.

The Disciples of Jesus received their Spiritual-Birthright Inheritance, and therefore were presented with the Miracle-Gifts and Graces of Holy Apostleship. Judas, in his betrayal of Jesus, failed to qualify for the receiving of his Spiritual-Birthright Inheritance.

The Christ seeks to lift men's souls to the heights of comprehending the myriad wonders of the Universe. The Antichrist seeks to keep man earthbound. The Christ works to inspire individuals to behold their Spiritual Birthright as a Map of the Universe, a Treasure Chest of Cosmos-realities, an endless Reservoir of Grace and Truth. The Antichrist tries to come between each person and his God-given Spiritual Birthright. Whenever a student of the higher life permits the Antichrist to plant doubts in his heart and mind regarding God, Jesus or his Living Teacher, each doubt becomes as a destructive cell that causes unhappiness and suffering. Like Esau and Judas, the student infected with the destructive cells of doubt loses a priceless opportunity to claim his Spiritual-Birthright Inheritance.

> *A good man leaveth an inheritance to his children's children: and the wealth of the sinner is laid up for the just.*
>
> *—Proverbs 13:22*

A student who turns away from the spiritual Path disqualifies himself from major Grace-Inheritances. In such instances, the Teacher and faithful students receive certain Inheritances rejected by the student. This may be likened to the members of a family who receive an inheritance. If one of the heirs fails to qualify by refusing to accept the terms of the inheritance, the inheritance is then divided among the family members who are willing to comply. So it is in the higher life: If any member of one's spiritual family, a fellow student, rejects the Scriptural statutes and discipleship disciplines, certain forfeited Inheritances of Grace are given to his Teacher and co-disciples.

> *For whosoever hath, to him shall be given, and he shall have more abundance: but whosoever hath not, from him shall be taken away even that he hath.*
> —*St. Matthew 13:12*

REDEEMING OF LOST GRACE

> *And bring hither the fatted calf, and kill it; and let us eat, and be merry: For this my son was dead, and is alive again; he was lost, and is found. And they began to be merry.*
> —*St. Luke 15:23,24*

Through the Redeeming Grace of God, one who repents and rededicates his life to Virtue and Truth may once again begin the process of qualifying for the progressive stages of Grace-Inheritances. A truly contrite heart restores one's equilibrium on the Path of Righteousness—and he experiences the Merciful Love of God manifesting in his life and being through the *redeeming* of Grace-Inheritances previously forfeited through willful transgressions of Holy Law. The Miracle of God's Love also provides one with endless opportunities to redeem Cycles of Grace-Inheritances forfeited in past lives!

The Prodigal Son, regardless of his wayward life, remained

an heir of his Father, the King. The Mercy of God extends to all penitents the opportunity to reclaim all inheritances rejected through sin, negligence and irreverence. Through sincere repentance, contrition, confession, restitution, daily worship, and dedication to the Commandments of God and the Ethics of Jesus, one may reclaim all lost inheritances of this life and past lives — and also receive the *new* Cycles of Inheritance that come to the just, the righteous, the reverent.

To begin to receive the Inheritances of Grace forfeited in past lives as well as in the present life is a time of great joy and rejoicing. Thereafter, one begins his union with the Eternal Mercy, Dimensional Love and Infinite Grace of God!

> *I have blotted out, as a thick cloud, thy transgressions, and, as a cloud, thy sins: return unto Me; for I have redeemed thee.*
>
> *—Isaiah 44:22*

KEY CYCLES ON THE PATH

> *Take fast hold of instruction; let her not go: keep her; for she is thy life.*
>
> *—Proverbs 4:13*

The greatest inheritance one may receive from God during his quest for Enlightenment is to be guided to a Living Teacher. A student's attitudes toward his Teacher determine his receiving or not receiving the progressive blessings of Grace-Inheritances.

An alert Truth-seeker knows that an Anointed Teacher is a rare blessing of God's Grace. Such students receive the priceless Inheritances of Grace as long as they express gratitude for instruction and are reverently obedient toward each Law and Commandment of God. When an aspirant remains faithful to the Commandments and to his Teacher's instruction, his Grace-Inheritances flow into his life and being in key Cycles. Some of these Cycles are:

1. Each Sabbath Day . . . a seven-day Cycle.

2. Each New Moon . . . a 29.5 day Cycle.

3. Each Full Moon . . . a 29.5 day Cycle.

4. Each Class conducted by one's Teacher.

5. Each Tithe given to God with love.

6. Each period of daily-worship of God through Prayer and Meditation.

7. Each Sacramental Fast.

8. Each Birth Day.

9. Each Holy Day.

10. Each Spiritual Pilgrimage.

11. Each Solstice and Equinox.

12. Each Planetary Cycle.

The Cycles of the Sun, the Moon and the Planets have been ordained since the beginning of the Solar System. These Immutable Cycles are part of the Great Covenant between God and man. When one begins to revere these mighty Cycles and to fulfill their sacred purposes, he receives the Gifts and Graces that constitute each Cyclic Inheritance.

As one comes into *timing* with his Teacher's instruction and with the harmony of the Holy Commandments, he begins his first receiving of Spiritual-Birthright Inheritances. Soul-gifts, talents and skills manifest in his being as steady increases of Grace through the Cycles of the Moon, the Sun and the Planets.

The acceleration and magnification of Grace-Inheritances occur in the Cycle of the Four Seasons: the Vernal Equinox, the Summer Solstice, the Autumnal Equinox and the Winter Solstice. The Grace-Inheritances received through the Cycle of the Four Seasons increase profoundly after each *Year* of dedicated service to God. Therefore, Grace-Inheritances are cumulative from Year to Year, Season to Season, New Moon to New Moon, Full Moon to Full Moon, Sabbath to Sabbath, Tithe to Tithe, Daily Worship to Daily Worship. *"Draw nigh unto God, and He will draw nigh unto you." (James 4:8)*

> *And it shall come to pass, that from one new moon to another, and from one sabbath to another, shall all flesh come to worship before me, saith the Lord.*
>
> *—Isaiah 66:23*

The New Moon Cycle and the Sabbath Cycle are significant Cycles of Inheritance through which one earns the Crown of his Spiritual Birthright. Students, devotees, initiates and Teachers progress through these all-important Cycles of the Moon and the Sabbath.

A closeness with God is established through one's dedication to the Sabbath-Day Commandment and Covenant. All Cycles of Inheritance related to one's Spiritual Birthright are perpetuated and prospered as long as he is faithful to the Sabbath-Day Commandment and the other Scriptural Statutes.

If a student of the higher life fails to fulfill the Sabbath Day of worship and devotion to God, he interrupts the cyclic continuity of his dedication, thereby removing himself from the protection of the Sabbath Covenant. The fall from the Grace of God begins the moment one turns his heart and mind away from the Ten Commandments and the Commandments of Love.

*Ye shall keep my sabbaths, and reverence my
sanctuary: I am the Lord.*
—*Leviticus 19:30*

"A man's foes shall be they of his own household." (St. Matthew 10:36) An enlightened Teacher constantly seeks to inspire each student to come into timing with God's Grace. In many instances, the family members of a student provide the tests that precede each Grace-Inheritance. Students who transcend the obstacles placed in their path by family members receive their Grace-Inheritances from God. Students who love one or more family members more than God and Jesus fail to qualify for the Cycles of Spiritual-Birthright Inheritance.

*He that loveth father or mother more than me is
not worthy of me: and he that loveth son or
daughter more than me is not worthy of me.*
—*St. Matthew 10:37*

In some instances, family members will deliberately try to interfere with one's dedication to worship God on the Sabbath Day. If the Sabbath-Day Commandment is fulfilled, regardless of the objections encountered in one's family, one proves worthy in the sight of God. If one yields to the selfish desires of family members, and fails to worship God each Sabbath Day, he has refused to accept the *terms* of the Grace-Inheritances — that is, the fulfilling of the Ten Commandments and the Commandments of Love. *"If ye love me, keep my commandments."* (St. John 14:15)

A family member who objects to a student's tithing to God is a test that faces some probationers. If a student fails to give God an honest tithe due to family pressure or his own lack of faith, he fails to qualify for the Cycles of Spiritual-Birthright Inheritance. Such students become laggards on the Path; inevitably, their family problems and personal problems mount. They have yet to learn that by rejecting God's Law of Tithing, they are also rejecting their Grace-Inheritances.

The Cycles of Spiritual-Birthright Inheritances begin the moment one turns to God with a wholehearted love — a love that transcends love for self, family, nation, race, religion. To love God as the Eternal and Absolute Truth, the Omnipresent Creator, is to meet each test with dignity, honor and integrity. Grace-Inheritances come not to the weak in faith; they come to the strong in faith. *"According to your faith be it unto you." (St. Matthew 9:29)*

The twelve Zodiacal Constellations surrounding the Solar System are mighty sources of Inheritances for mankind. The Zodiacal-Constellations Inheritances are received as blessings from God through the twelve Zodiacal Prototypes on Earth. For example, when one proves faithful to the Commandments, the Creator blesses him in numerous ways through persons representing the twelve Zodiacal Prototypes: Aries, Taurus, Gemini, Cancer, Leo, Virgo, Libra, Scorpio, Sagittarius, Capricorn, Aquarius and Pisces. These blessings are *Constellation-Grace Inheritances* through the Prototypes. In time, one's love for God and love for the twelve types of persons on Earth produce *Prototypal Illuminations*.

Each of the Ten Commandments has its Cyclic Inheritances. The Commandment of Tithing has its Cyclic Inheritances. Each Commandment of Love has its Cyclic Inheritances. Thus, a sincere and faithful servant of God attains the Cycles of Inheritance as bountiful harvests of Grace. This is the true State of Grace sought by all who love God, His Commandments and His Cosmos Creation.

> *To learn of his origins, man must look to the starry heavens. To learn of his Inheritances, he must look to the Commandments as Cosmos-Energies.*

THE NEW COVENANT AND THE CHRIST-MIND INITIATE

*Blessed be the God and Father of our Lord Jesus
Christ, which according to his abundant mercy
hath begotten us again unto a lively hope by the
resurrection of Jesus Christ from the dead, To an
inheritance incorruptible, and undefiled, and that
fadeth not away, reserved in heaven for you, Who
are kept by the power of God through faith unto
salvation ready to be revealed in the last time.*
—1 Peter 1:3–5

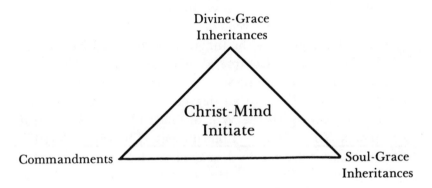

The *New Covenant* is a Covenant of Cyclic Inheritances
made manifest through faith, love and reverent service to God
in the Name of His Son. The New Covenant is a Cosmos-
Creation Covenant. As one matures spiritually, he lovingly
embraces the Cosmos as the Body of God. Even as Saint
Francis of Assisi looked upon "brother sun" and "sister
moon," so does an enlightened worshipper of God think of
himself as part of the family of celestial bodies.

*"For who hath known the mind of the Lord, that he may
instruct him? But we have the mind of Christ." (1 Corinthians
2:16)* The Christ-Mind Initiate is at one with God as the
Creator of the Earth and the Universe. Through this sanctifed

union or marriage with God, his vision extends from the planet Earth to the starry Cosmos.

An aspirant who proves to be a good steward of the Commandments of God receives inheritances of *Soul-Grace*. If he proves to be a wise steward of Soul-Grace Inheritances, he receives *Divine-Grace Inheritances*. Every earnest devotee of the Lord Christ embraces the Commandments of God with all his love, thereby becoming an heir to the spiritual riches of the New Covenant.

The Commandments establish *cycles* in one's life: cycles of worship, cycles of good works, cycles of study, cycles of creativity. These cycles inspired by Holy Law bring one into perfect timing with the Cycles of the Soul. Through the Cycles of the Soul, one receives the Inheritances of Past-Lives Grace.

The Cycles of the Commandments and the Cycles of the Soul are *one*. Through these Sacred Cycles, one unites with the Christ — the Door to all degrees of Divine Grace. The Christ, working with the Will of God, blesses His faithful sheep with Divine-Grace Inheritances. These priceless Inheritances also are received in Cycles.

Through the Cycles of Divine-Grace Inheritances, one becomes a Christ-Mind Initiate. God-Realization comes to Christ-Mind Initiates in the State of Divine-Inheritances Grace through the New Covenant.

A Truth-seeker should revere all Celestial Cycles established by the Creator. The splendor of the Cycles is the foundation for the Pillars of the Temple of Soul-Beauty and Illumination-Grace.

> *One should on entering the Path seek to interrelate, to interconnect, to blend and to harmonize that he may enter into his whole and complete inheritance as imaged into the Constant.*
>
> *—Ann Ree Colton*

The Holy Flow and the Three Centerings

> Grace is necessary to salvation, free will is equally
> so; but grace in order to give salvation, free will in
> order to receive it.
>
> —St. Bernard, c. 1150

> Only those are deprived of grace, who place in
> themselves an obstacle to grace.
>
> —St. Thomas Aquinas, 1260

The *Path* of the higher life represents different *Flows*. The Spirit of God moves each probationer and aspirant into ever-increasing Flows of Grace and Truth until the Divine Marriage is accomplished.

All Flows are *Holy*. All Flows are energy-currents that move one into the progressive states of God's Quickening Light and Love.

The Flow of Truth from time immemorial is the *Dharmic Flow*. The Dharmic Flow includes all Holy Flows between Heaven and Earth. The Dharma is an unceasing Flow of Sacred Truths that continually presses upon the hearts and minds of persons throughout the world. Gradually, the Dharma finds receptive hearts and minds through which to manifest holy instruction; to heal races, nations and continents; and to keep the human spirit ever attuned to the Will of God creating the Universe.

The Dharmic Flow moves from Heaven to Earth: the visible heaven of Stars, Constellations and Galaxies; and the invisible Heaven of Great Beings and Holy Presences. The Dharmic Flow is distributed to the world of man through the Mediation of the Holy Ghost; in this, the Dharmic Flow becomes the *Holy-Ghost Flow*.

Whereas the Dharmic Flow works in the Greater Cycles,

the Holy-Ghost Flow translates these powerful energies into cycles and degrees of energy to which the hearts and minds of men can relate. The various states and stages of Enlightenment occur under the direct supervision of the Holy Ghost — thus, Jesus said, *"Receive ye the Holy Ghost." (St. John 20:22)*

The Holy Ghost works with and through the Commandments of God. Therefore, only those who are dedicated to the Commandments of God become the recipients of the Holy Ghost. Consequently, those who receive the Holy Ghost become devotees and Teachers of the Dharma.

The *degree* to which one is dedicated to the Commandments of God determines the degree of Holy-Ghost Flow in his life and being. The Door to God's World of Grace and Truth remains open to hearts and minds sanctified by the Presence of God within His Laws and Commandments.

The *Commandment Flow* is an ascending energy that draws one into the different levels of Soul-Grace. In time, a sincere devotee becomes centered in the Grace of the *Soul Flow*. To be centered in the Soul Flow is to experience the Love and Mercy of God in their dimensional grandeur. This high State of Grace prepares one for a more quickened State of Grace called the *Archetypal Flow*.

The Archetypal Flow centers one in the Heart of God through the Divine-Marriage Anointing. The Holy Ghost provides the Great Gifts through which God is glorified, thereby enabling the anointed servant of God to express the *"gifts of the Holy Ghost." (Hebrews 2:4)*

An enlightened Teacher's wisdom and knowledge come through the Archetypal Flow. Such Teachers seek to shepherd probationer-students into the Commandment Flow. As a student becomes centered in the Commandment Flow, he moves quickly into the Soul Flow. In the Soul Flow of Grace and Truth, works and creations of Soul-Beauty abound, for the student is beginning to unite with the Constant of God sealed into his Soul.

DHARMIC FLOW

HOLY GHOST FLOW

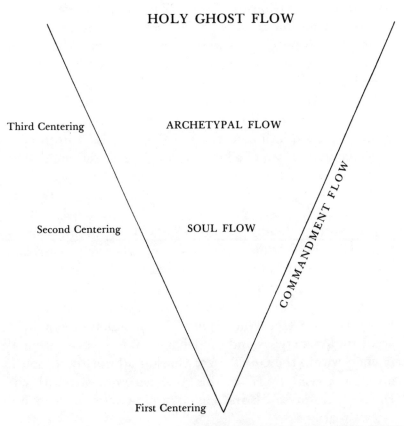

Third Centering   ARCHETYPAL FLOW

Second Centering   SOUL FLOW

First Centering

THE HOLY FLOW AND THE
THREE CENTERINGS

When a Truth-seeker unites totally with the Constant of God in his Soul, he becomes a Teacher moving within the Christ-Mind Velocities, Versatilities and Voltages of the Archetypal Flow. The Archetypal Flow produces the state of Illumination called *God-Realization.*

The Archetypal Flow, being *within* the Dharma, is a constant revealer of Dharmic Truths. The *New Covenant* is the New-Era Dharma coming to the world through the Lord Jesus. The New Covenant is man's link with the Outer Universe of Celestial Creations and the Inner Universe of Timeless Realities.

Every seeker after Truth must travel the same Path. The Path, consisting of pure Commandment-energies, takes one through the initiating currents of the Soul Flow until he is purged and cleansed of all impurities of heart and mind. The Path then places him in the quickened grace-energy currents of the Archetypal Flow. In this, the Path becomes the *Archetypal Path.*

All devotees should pray to move with the momentum of God's Holy Flow. The rapidity of their progress is assured as soon as they attain correct attitudes and establish their sincerity, loyalty and integrity in the sight of God.

After one earns the Holy-Ghost Baptismal Anointing, all Flows become *One* Holy Flow. The Commandments, the Soul, the Archetypes and the Dharma reveal their essential oneness within the One Plan of God for all worlds, all souls, all Cosmos Creations. In this, one becomes one with the Divine Omnipresence and His Majestic Cycles of Pure and Holy Creations.

To Flow with the Universal Harmony is to express the Holy Flow while in Heaven or on Earth. The Holy Flow is the Dance to the Music of God's Love caressing and creating all Stars and Galaxies. To be in rhythm with the Holy Flow is to know God, to serve Him, and to glorify His Holy Name.

In the higher life, there are three major *Centerings* that

correlate to the different Flows. The *First Centering* is attained through the fulfillment of the Laws and Commandments of God as an unwavering spiritual dedication. In this, one becomes centered in the Grace, Mercy and Love of God within the Commandment Flow.

The *Second Centering* relates to the Soul and its Gifts and Powers. One who attains this Centering experiences the Grace, Mercy and Love of God within the Soul Flow. First-Heaven Inspiration Seals and Second-Heaven Realization Seals open and bless the devotee with wisdom, understanding and virtue.

The *Third Centering* pertains to the Archetypes of God in the Third Heaven. To be centered in the Archetypal Flow is a high degree of Grace received through the Spirit of God, producing the Holy-Ghost Gifts of Healing, Prophecy and Revelation. The Christ-Mind Apostle has attained the Third Centering, and thus represents Jesus in the world as a Cosmos-Disciple at one with the Harmonious Creation of the Universe.

The generosity and magnanimity of God are transmitted to man through the Cyclic Flows of Grace-Inheritances presented by the energies of the Sun, the Moon and the Planets. These Inheritances lead to even greater Inheritances of Grace: Inheritances from the Stars and Inheritances from the Galaxies.

The Christ, as Mediator between God and man, purges, initiates and illuminates His sheep. The New-Covenant Inheritances received by His faithful sheep are indelibly recorded in the heart, mind and soul. Through the rewards and blessings of these Inheritances, one becomes an anointed and enlightened servant of God.

How much more shall the blood of Christ, who through the eternal Spirit offered himself without spot to God, purge your conscience from dead works to serve the living God? And for this cause he is the mediator of the new testament, that by means of death, for the redemption of the transgressions that were under the first testament, they which are called might receive the promise of eternal inheritance.

—Hebrews 9:14,15

The mind in Christ is fed and nourished by the Cosmos-Energies of sister and brother Stars, sister and brother Galaxies. The next 7,000 years will see the establishing of the Christ Mind on Earth—the Mind that will enable man to receive the New-Covenant Inheritances. These Inheritances will establish man as an ethical citizen of the Cosmos. No longer earthbound by resistances to the Commandments, he will unite with the Glory and Love of God within His Wise Plan of Cyclic Inheritances.

"And every one that hath forsaken houses, or brethren, or sisters, or father, or mother, or wife, or children, or lands, for my name's sake, shall receive an hundredfold, and shall inherit everlasting life." (St. Matthew 19:29) The inheritance of "everlasting life" is the Eternal-Life Consciousness. The Eternal-Life Consciousness is the Galaxy Consciousness, the New-Covenant Consciousness. This exalted Consciousness is one's Spiritual Birthright. Through the Eternal-Life Consciousness, one unites with the Glory of God in the Sun, the Moon, the Planets, the Stars and the Galaxies.

Grace is so gracious and so graciously seizes on our hearts to draw them, that it in no way offends the liberty of our will.

—St. Francis of Sales, 1607

Every virtuous act done for Christ's sake gives us the grace of the Holy Spirit, but most of all is this given through prayer; for prayer is somehow always in our hands as an instrument for acquiring the grace of the Spirit.

—St. Seraphim of Sarov (1759-1833)

Saturn, the Teacher

Saturn represents self-discipline and the Teacher.
—*Ann Ree Colton*

"God is Love." (St. John 4:8) God is the Love in the Soul, the Love in the Star, the Love in the Universe. When one loves, he has the key to union with God as Love in Souls, in Stars and in Galaxies.

One must be able to love his fellow men as creations of God before he can love the Stars and the Galaxies as creations of God. Love unites Souls on Earth; love unites one with the Stars; love unites one with the totality of Creation occurring within the Universe.

Each Planet is a manifestation of God's Love. The Planets move in synchronized harmony around the Sun. When one learns the Cycles of the Planets, he is learning the Mathematics of God pertaining to the Solar System and to the Soul. Man, as a Soul, is responding every moment to the Movement, Energies and Cycles of the Sun, the Moon and the Planets. The *Inheritances* mentioned in the Holy Bible include Gifts from the Celestial Bodies and their Cyclic Energy-Processes.

Each Planet makes one complete cycle or revolution around the Sun in the following period of Time:

Mercury—88 days
Venus—224.7 days
Earth—365 days
Mars—687 days
Jupiter—11.86 years

Saturn — 29.46 years
Uranus — 84 years
Neptune — 165 years
Pluto — 248 years

The planet Saturn, as a Teacher, works with and through all who are dedicated to the mighty Principle of Teaching. Saturn's Cycle of 29.46 years is an Initiatory Cycle during which a spiritual aspirant may evolve from student to devotee to initiate to Teacher. If a Truth-seeker proves faithful to God, he receives the Inheritance of Saturn's Gift: the Mantle of the Teacher. This occurs in his 30th year on the Path of Virtue.

Jesus began His Ministry in His 30th year, thereby fulfilling a Saturn Cycle. The supernal energies of God's Love blessing the world through the Cycle of Saturn placed upon the shoulders of Jesus the Mantle of the World Teacher, Saviour and Messiah.

The rare wisdom of Jesus and His versatile miracles revealed an enlightened knowledge of Saturn's energy-processes. The Gift of Miracles and other Apostolic Gifts are passed onto those who teach and heal under the Mantle of Jesus. Miracles are the utilization of little-known energies on accelerated levels of light and law.

Saturn, the Teacher, inspires one to work with the Image of God within the soul. It also inspires him to work with the Image of God within the souls of others. In this, one becomes a true Teacher of God's Word, blessed with the cherished Gift of Understanding and the royal Gift of Prophecy through Time's overcoming.

Judas was tested, and fell victim to the tester. Peter was tested, and was preserved. Thomas was tested for his faith, and passed the test. So is each follower of the Christ tested. Those who remain steadfast on the Way of Righteousness and Holiness receive monumental blessings, quickenings and anointings from God through the sacred Cycle of Saturn whose light brightens the heart and the heavens.

The Saturn Cycle of 29.46 years, as a Grace-Inheritance Cycle, begins the moment one's heart and mind reach toward God through sincere dedication and wholehearted love. If a probationer proves obedient to instruction received from his Living Teacher, Saturn's initiatory energies begin the purification and spiritualization of his attitudes, motives, feelings, thoughts and actions. Saturn, the Teacher, teaches him through his Living Teacher, through Sacred Scripture, and through every person and event in his life. Each friend, family member, business associate, and co-disciple represents many lessons in love and ethic.

Each lesson experienced in the day's actions and in the night's dreams is a lesson presented by Saturn. The cyclic rhythm of Saturn is a *Teaching Rhythm* affecting each level of life: racial, national, tribal, family, religion, individual. Mankind is in the continuous flow of Learning through Saturn's Light.

The Glory and Love of God within the powerful planet Saturn begin to be comprehended through the spiritual sensitivity attained in Sacramental Meditation and other devotional practices. Daily worship, study and selfless service prepare the probationer for the time when he will wear the Mantle of the Teacher as a Gift from Saturn.

The Christ liberates through Truth and Love; the Antichrist seeks to place persons into bondage. Each individual on Earth is given the *choice* to learn from the Christ, the World Teacher, or to learn from the Antichrist. To learn from the Christ is to learn through love and logic. If one resists learning through love and logic, he experiences learning through pain and suffering caused by sins of omission and commission.

Learning is the purpose of human life on Earth. The Tree of Knowledge is for all souls to gather the fruits of learning.

The sweet fruit of learning and the bitter fruit of learning are growing on the same Tree of Knowledge. When one loves learning, he eats the sweet fruit; when one resists learning, he eats the bitter fruit. The Christ teaches through the higher energies of Saturn. The Antichrist (Satan) teaches through the lower energies of Saturn. The Christ teaches the teachable, the righteous, the moral. The Antichrist teaches the self-willed, the unrighteous, the immoral. Whereas Saturn's higher energies provide ethical Teachers with an Illumination-feast at the Lord's Table, Saturn's lower energies provide stern disciplines for the selfish and reproofs for the wayward.

The learning process enables an earnest devotee to eventually discern the difference between right and wrong, good and evil. In this, he becomes a servant of God fortified by the Holy Gift of Discernment.

The Mantle of the Teacher is woven by the threads of numerous lessons learned during Saturn's Cycle. From these necessary lessons and initiatory struggles, the Mantle of the Teacher is gradually woven.

The 30th year of faithful service to God marks the ending of one Saturn Cycle and the beginning of a new Saturn Cycle.

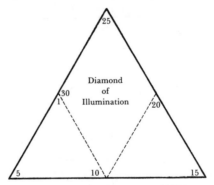

After thirty years on the Path of Virtue, a faithful servant of God inherits the Gift of Saturn's Cycle: The Teacher's Mantle.*

*Chart by Ann Ree Colton and Jonathan Murro

MERCURY: THE SUN'S SCRIBE

Mercury's Cycle: 88 days. The swift-moving planet Mercury fulfills an 88-day cycle around the Sun. Mercury, the planet closest to the Sun, was called by the ancients "the Sun's scribe."

Mercury's Gift of Grace-Inheritances relates to one's receiving priceless Christ-Mind skills and aptitudes. One who earns the Teacher's Mantle responds to Mercury's energy-influences as Christ-Mind Illuminations during the four Seasonal Tides. Each Season, about 90 days in length, approximates one complete Mercury Cycle.

Students who come into timing with their Teacher's Grace-Inheritances Cycles come under the direct Blessing-Power of God manifesting through Mercury's orbit and the correlating Seasonal Cycles of the Solstices and the Equinoxes. The Winter Solstice, the Vernal Equinox, the Summer Solstice and the Autumnal Equinox, occurring each year with rhythmic regularity, prepare an earnest devotee for the time when he will receive the Christ-Mind as a Benediction from God's Love through the planet Mercury.

One Spiritual-Birthright Inheritance leads to another Inheritance after one establishes himself within the Constant of God's Love. The *seals* on precious treasures of Truth and Grace open through union with the Spirit of God blessing the world through the Cycles of Saturn and Mercury. To move with the Grace-Flow of the fast-moving Mercury and to be stabilized within the Grace-Flow of the slow-moving Saturn is to serve the world-need as a Scribe for God. To such rare souls, God reveals inspired prophecies, realizations and revelations that prepare mankind for the future. To leave to coming generations an inheritance of hope and wisdom is the joy of the Anointed Teacher graced with Christ-Mind skills and prophetic vision.

As a Truth-seeker climbs to a higher rung on the Ladder

of the Spiritual Life, he unites with higher degrees of energy being emitted by the Sun, the Moon and each Planet. Each degree of solar, lunar and planetary energy pertains to a degree of God's Grace and Love. Thus, each ascending step on the Ladder is a time of Inheritance that enables one to commune more freely and fully with God's Holy Spirit.

As one breaks free from Earth-bondages, he can perceive the Truth more clearly. God, as Truth, can begin to be discerned only after one proves his love for Pure Truth more than love for persons or things.

JUPITER AND THE BRHASPATI CYCLE

Jupiter's Cycle: 11.86 years. In Sanskrit, one meaning of the word "Brhaspati" is *Jupiter.* The planet Jupiter requires 11.86 years to make one revolution around the Sun. The ancient Hindus called five completed cycles of Jupiter a *Brhaspati Cycle.* Each 60-year Brhaspati Cycle was considered to be an important timing for the world.

Jupiter, the largest planet in the Solar System, has invaluable Gifts or Inheritances that manifest in 12-year periods. For the spiritual initiate, the *expanding consciousness* is a reality through Jupiter's energy influences. The soul's largesse becomes part of one's being, engendering a magnanimous love-nature, a deepening of faith, a broadening of mental attributes, a quickening of soul-treasures.

The Virtue of Jupiter becomes part of one's being when his works are devoted to God and man. As one proves faithful to Scriptural formats for living, worship and creating, Jupiter's light enables him to move ever-closer to the voluminous power of the Godhead.

"And of his fulness have all we received, and grace for grace." (St. John 1:16) The *fulness* of Jesus is a fulness blessed by Jupiter and its wondrous Gifts for man. The fulness of

grace experienced by one who attains union with God is an ever-expanding fulness, enabling him to understand secrets and mysteries of Time and Space.

As Jupiter moves, one evolves; as Jupiter reveals God's Glory within its Cycle, one becomes increasingly virtuous, righteous and enlightened. The Principle of Magnification, the Principle of Divine Expansion, the Principle of Holy Creation, and other mighty Principles are known and understood by the illumined Seer and Saint who completes a 60-year Brhaspati Cycle in faithful service to the Creator. The dignity of the Dharma is preserved in each age and time by those who bless the Earth with their love and their wisdom.

Brhaspati is also the name of a Great Being revered in Eastern Scripture. He is affectionately known as the Lord of Prayer. In some areas of the world, he is called *Father Jupiter*. Some refer to him as *the Venerable One*, the Great Immortal who works to prepare devotees for the Illumination-Anointing of the Divine Marriage.

Jupiter's Cycles of Inheritance provide an earnest Truth-seeker with physical and spiritual prosperity. Past-lives of giving tithes and offerings to God bless one's present life with the flow of Providential Grace from God. The tithes and offerings given to God in one's present life and in coming lives will keep him centered in Jupiter's Gift of perpetual prosperity in body, heart, mind, soul and spirit.

VENUS

> *Venus is the planet-light of love, human and spiritual.*
>
> *—Ann Ree Colton*

Venus' Cycle: 224.7 days. Venus' Cycle of 224.7 days initiates all probationers on the Path of Virtue. The result of these initiations is a pure and holy love, thereby uniting one with the Glory of God in the Commandments of Love: Love for God, love for one's neighbor, love for one another, and love for one's enemies.

To be an heir of Christ is to be an heir of God's Love. The Sacrament of Communion received in Jesus' Name consecrates one's love, thereby qualifying him to receive Venus' Cycles of Inheritance.

Whereas Mars is a planet of cold, Venus is a planet of heat. As one progresses on the spiritual Path, his love-motives are refined by the fiery nature of Venus. *"Beloved, think it not strange concerning the fiery trial which is to try you." (1 Peter 4:12)*

When love is offended, it burns. The fiery trials experienced by devotee-initiates burn away the sins accumulated through the wrong use of love: lust, self-love, possessive love, love of man-made idols. One's failure to fulfill the vows of marital love and other offenses against the Love-Commandments are consumed in the fiery-trial initiations until one becomes a true devotee or disciple of the Christ. To become an earnest disciple of the Lord of Love, is to receive the love-surprises and love-creations through the Cycles of Inheritance from Venus.

Venus inspires one to return all blessings to God in the spirit of Holy Humility and Holy Poverty sanctified by Selfless Love. The Cyclic Inheritances from the planet Venus are Inheritances of Pure Love, which one may use in devoted service to God and his fellow man.

> *The Anointing Spirit of God manifests its mighty blessings through the planetary, solar and lunar energy-tides. One who is anointed by God is in a constant state of profound Grace-Inheritances. This is the nature of God's Love as it blesses, prospers and enlightens those who love Him.*

MARS

Mars' Cycle: 687 days. Mars, through its Cycle of 687 days, provides the Inheritances of Grace through which the Saints and their proteges may remain fortified in their Holy War against evil and unrighteousness.

Mars works with the energy-inheritances of the body and the soul. The harmonious energies that enable one to remain in constant service to God and to fulfill all spiritual dedications with effortless effort come through the Inheritance-Cycles of Mars.

The birth of intellectual genius or spiritual genius denotes grace from past lives being inherited in one's present life. Key energy-processes related to genius-accomplishments are under the jurisdiction of the planet Mars and the great Hierarch Blessing-Power through this neighboring planet.

Many persons have earned in previous lives the grace of intellectual brilliance; others have earned a spiritual intelligence. Through the soul's record, intellectual brilliance may reappear in one's present life — however, intellectual brilliance devoid of ethics and morality is dangerous to oneself and to others. Intellectual brilliance accompanied by love, compassion and benevolence blesses the world in outstanding ways.

The greatest contributions to the human spirit come through those endowed with a spiritual intelligence. A spiritual intelligence expressed in service to God leaves to the world many works of beauty, wisdom and truth. Whatever a servant of God inherits from the Soul and from the Creator through the Cycles of the Sun, the Moon and the Planets blesses the world in unique and profound ways.

The greatest Inheritances of Grace include the Inheritances of *Conscience Energy-Units, Virtue Energy-Units, Logic Energy-Units,* and *Love Energy-Units.* These important

Energy-Units continue to add their light to the consciousness mind during one's quest for Enlightenment. The heart and mind are transformed through dramatic surges of Soul-Grace manifesting as Energy-Units of Conscience, Virtue, Logic and Love.

To become Commandment-minded and worship-minded immediately begins one's union with the higher energies of Mars that activate energy-treasures of grace from the soul and the spirit.

URANUS, NEPTUNE AND PLUTO: THE GALAXY-GATE PLANETS

Uranus' Cycle: 84 years.
Neptune's Cycle: 165 years.
Pluto's Cycle: 248 years.

Mankind progresses toward Soul-Liberation through the Cycles of the Planets and their timely blessings upon the human spirit as a whole. Man is not doomed — for he is in a state of perpetual progression with major periods of Soul-Liberation made possible by Planetary Inheritance-Cycles.

The Cycles of the Soul and the Cycles of the Planets are always in perfect harmony. The synchronization of all inner and outer Cycles is part of God's Perfect Plan. The past lives, present life and future lives of each individual always fulfill the Synchronization of Cycles. To trust in God is to trust in the mathematics of His ordained Cycles: Solar, Lunar, Planetary, Galactic. All Stars, Clusters of Stars, Galaxies and Clusters of Galaxies are in continuous synchronization. When the heart and mind are ready, the soul reveals the secrets of its own synchronization as related to the synchronization of the celestial bodies in the Universe.

Piece by piece, the puzzle of Eternal Life is being solved. As heirs of a Wise and Kind Heavenly Father, men are discovering the secrets of Synchronized Cycles. This knowledge is drawing them ever upward into the awareness of the Cycles occurring in Outer Space and the Cycles of the Soul within the Inner Kingdom. When man understands the Synchronization of Cycles, he will experience another level of Inheritance. No longer resisting the Creator, he will work in synchronized harmony with the Universe — a harmony made possible by the Cyclic Inheritances received from the Glory of God in the Sun, the Moon, the Planets, the Stars, the Galaxies.

The Galaxy-Gate Planets, Uranus, Neptune and Pluto, have longer Cycles that provide special Grace-Inheritances from past lives; they also produce great blessings in the future lives of those who worship God and keep His Commandments in their present lives. Those who are persecuted or martyred for righteousness' sake will be the beneficiaries of spiritual riches in their coming lives. The *timing* of their lives on Earth — past, present and future — is in perfect synchronized harmony with the Galaxy-Gate Planets and their sweeping orbits around the Sun.

Each of the three outer planets in the Solar System is man's link with God's Glory in the Universe beyond the Sun and beyond the Milky Way Galaxy. The knowledge of the Cosmos occurs in dramatic revelations timed by the Cycles of Uranus (84 years), Neptune (165 years), and Pluto (248 years) as they bequeath to receptive individuals the wisdom-treasures earned in past lives and also new realizations regarding the present and the future. Key Cycles activated by Uranus, Neptune and Pluto provide anointed servants of God with the rewards and inheritances of Cosmos Illumination-Grace.

A Gift of Uranus is to give one understanding of the *electricities* of the soul and the spirit. Uranus sheds light on light. The light of the soul is a bright and powerful light; to receive of this light, one must become spiritually insulated. Virtues and love provide the insulation for the soul's light to move freely and safely in the heart and mind. Uranus works to insulate man so that the insulation provided by virtues and love will enable him to understand the Electricity of God's Spirit which illuminates all Stars and Galaxies.

Neptune's Gift comes to man as Cyclic Inheritances of Creative Imagination. The imagination blossoms as a beautiful flower under the Grace-Quickenings of God's Spirit through the energy-influences of Neptune. The imagination of man looks to the starry heavens — and the human spirit ponders its placement in the Universal Plan of God. Neptune turns the eyes of man starward, freeing him from bondage to earthbound thoughts. Neptune points toward distant Galaxies, assuring man of rhythmic strides of progress and soul-liberation through Imagination. The Cycles of Neptune bless every physical and spiritual art and science with the stimulation of new creations.

The certainty of Creation fulfilling itself on Earth and in Heaven is a never-ending certainty — for God, the Creator, speaks *His Word* through the Great Cycles of the Universe.

Pluto, new to the minds of men (1930), is an old friend. The intensity of Pluto's energy-influences is a subtle energy until it unclogs the subconscious of all manner of emotional debris and clears away the sin-shadows in the mind. The Glory of God in Pluto holds the key for man to discover his own worth and dignity as a son of God.

The Cycles of Inheritance received from Pluto's placement in the Solar System light the way for the Soul of man to comprehend to Soul of the Universe.

THE SUN AND THE SOUL

> *The mighty God, even the Lord hath spoken,*
> *and called the earth from the rising of the sun un-*
> *to the going down thereof.* —*Psalm 50:1*

Courtesy of Virgil Smith and Silas Elash; also photograph on page 191.

The Sun's Gift is a regulated and harmonious supply of energy for all physical, emotional, mental and spiritual needs and expressions. The Soul blesses through Solar Cycles; purification of the Soul's Record results in the continuous flow of Soul-Grace blessed by the Sun's energies.

The Sun's Gift increases each Solar Year, thereby enabling the Christ-Mind Initiate and Teacher to live within the synchronized harmony of the Soul's Grace-Flow and the Sun's Archetypal Grace-Flow. This synchronization of Cycles—Solar, Lunar and Planetary—enables one to serve God as a revelator of *Archetypal Truths.*

The Sun holds the key to the Third Heaven, wherein the Creator has sealed His Archetypes for the creation of the Solar System. To be initiated through the Solar Cycles is to qualify to receive knowledge blessing the world from the Third Heaven. To receive this priceless knowledge is to be co-atom to Jesus—and to minister and serve in the world as His appointed Apostle. To represent Jesus in the world is to be as a Sun radiating healing, hope, truth, wisdom, light, grace and love. Thus, all who serve God in Jesus' Name are as Suns whose light dispels darkness, and whose joy inspires faith in the perfection of God's Love and Mercy.

The Gift of the Sun is Constancy. To inherit the Gift of Constancy during the Sun's Cycles is to learn of the Constant of God as the Unifier of all Suns. To unite with the Glory of God in the Sun is to be graced with the key to understanding the eternal truths and cardinal constants being expressed by all Stars and Galaxies.

Sunspot activity fulfills an 11-year cycle, reaching a peak in the 22nd year. These key cycles regarding the Sun's energy-dynamics correlate to the mathematics of God within the soul and its cycles. In the spiritual sciences, 11 is the number of physical mastery; 22, the number of spiritual mastery.

THE MOON AND THE SOUL'S RECORD

> *He appointed the Moon for seasons.*
> —*Psalm 104:19*

The Moon, in its Cycle of 29.5 days around the Earth, is as the Finger of God pointing to the Soul's Record. The weaknesses and strengths inherited from past lives are magnified by the Moon during its various phases. The New Moon and Full Moon are heightened periods of magnification, revealing one's virtues and faults. In time, as an aspirant on the Path of Virtue progresses spiritually, the Moon becomes a powerful activator of Soul-Grace, for the Finger of God, through the Moon's Cycle, removes the locks on the Treasure Chests of the Soul.

As long as one persists in evil-doing or wrong-doing, the Finger of God becomes a persistent accuser, using the Lunar Energy-tides to reveal one's faults and hypocrisies. When one becomes self-honest—and begins to work with God to overcome his faults, wrong attitudes and negative traits—the

Moon assists him to break free from the bondages caused by sin-offenses recorded in the soul's record of the present life and past lives.

The Moon's Cycle is synchronized with all other Solar-System Cycles involving the Planets and their Moons. The perfect interrelationship and interaction of these Cycles testify to God's Perfect Plan.

"There is one glory of the sun, and another glory of the moon, and another glory of the stars: for one star differeth from another star in glory." (1 Corinthians 15:41) In the higher life, one must unite with the Glory of God within the Moon, the Sun and the Planets. This occurs through initiatory cleansings and quickenings of the heart, mind and soul. A soul-record cleansed through repentance, contrition, confession and restitution enables one to remain centered and polarized within Soul-Grace and Divine Grace. Persons who prove their love for God each day are rare souls. As they attain a cleansed soul-record, they can begin to perceive the

Face of God smiling upon them through the cyclic energy-processes of the Sun, the Moon, the Planets, the Stars and the Galaxies.

Even as one unites with the Flow of Soul-Grace through union with the Glory of God in the Moon, so does he unite with the Flow of Archetypal Grace through union with the Glory of God within the Sun. Archetypal Grace provides one with the profound wisdom and perceptive vision of the Anointed Prophet and Revelator blessed by God and the Christ. Through Archetypal Grace, one communes with the Archetypes or Blueprints of the Earth's Creation as recorded in the Third Heaven.

Each Solar System has its Heaven. The Heaven of one Solar System enables one to unite with the Glory of God in the Heavens of other Solar Systems.

Spiritual knowledge of the Stars and Galaxies will come in future decades, centuries and ages through the Illumined Ones who will prove worthy in God's sight. All who love and serve in the spirit of true Apostleship under Christ — fulfilling the Commandments of God with reverence and joyful enthusiasm — will become the heirs of the Cycles of Inheritance through which come wisdom-truths regarding the distant Stars and Galaxies.

> *This verily, is the door of the heavenly world —*
> *that is, the moon. Whoever answers it, him it lets*
> *go further.*
>
> *— Upanishads*

EARTH

Earth's Cycle: 365 days. The planet Earth is releasing many inheritances to mankind as a whole and to each reverent individual through its Cycle of 365 days. As the Earth travels around the Sun, the Will of God is being fulfilled. No one can reverse or tamper with the Cycle of the Earth or any other Planetary Cycle. The Earth is a planet for the budding spirituality of man.

When one seeks to learn of God and to do His Will, the Earth's Gift of Inheritance-Cycles becomes a major contributor to his progress on all levels of evolvement. Each *birth day* for a true servant of God is a time of special significance in Heaven and on Earth. A birth day presents him with gifts from loved ones and friends; God and the Heavenly Host also bless him with Gifts and Graces on his birth day. For those who teach Scriptural truths regarding the reality of Heaven, each birth day marks a time of new quickenings of the soul's grace-record. These Gifts of Grace are timed to the Inheritance-Cycle of the planet Earth.

The system of Inheritances as ordained by God is a wondrous system. Each Inheritance received in its cyclic timing prepares one for coming Inheritances. As one prospers in Grace and Truth, he may then qualify for the *Greater* Inheritances. In this, he unites with the magnanimous Love of God that blesses His faithful servants with the spiritual riches of knowledge, wisdom, understanding, and other precious Gifts and Treasures.

To move in complete harmony with the Cycles of the Sun, the Moon and the Planets—and to qualify to receive their bountiful Inheritances—one must live each day in total dedication to God and His Commandments.

The Cycles of Inheritance affect the individual, families, nations, races and religions. Wherever individuals or masses of people express love for God and adhere to His Statutes, the Cycles of Inheritance are blessing, healing, enlightening.

Fasting, prayer and meditation observed by a group of worshippers produce mighty blessings for the group and for the world. These blessings come in their cyclic timings as the group proves consistent and conscientious.

The world is approaching the time when the Earth and all its inhabitants will be in a composite State of Grace. When this occurs, the planet Earth and its sister and brother planets will provide new expanses of Dimensional Grace and Galaxy Grace through their Cycles of Inheritance.

MARRIAGE-GRACE INHERITANCES

Marriage is honourable in all, and the bed undefiled.

—Hebrews 13:4

In the spiritual life, four major dates contribute mightily to one's progress toward God-Realization:

1. One's birth day. In each Seven-Year Cycle throughout life, Grace manifests in substantial measures when one begins his search for God at an early age.

2. The day one speaks his first sincere prayer of dedication to God. If one is blessed with a Living Teacher, the Teacher is part of his Grace-Inheritances received from God. To *inherit* an enlightened Teacher is the choicest Gift of Grace from God—for the Teacher holds the key to the student's receiving the Greater Inheritances of Grace and Truth.

3. If one is married, the day he speaks his Marriage Vows is the third major date in the spiritual life.

4. The day one receives the Divine-Marriage Anointing. Thereafter, he serves God as one of the Anointed, an Illumined Apostle of the Lord Jesus who qualifies for the cyclic blessings of Apostolic Inheritances that increase over the years.

The various Cycles of Inheritance are activated in different intervals throughout one's physical life, marital life, and spiritual life. As one progresses from devotee to initiate to Anointed Teacher, the Cycles of Grace-Inheritances increase profoundly. All Grace-Inheritances contribute to one's attaining the spiritual riches of the soul and the spirit. The State of Grace experienced by all loyal servants of God is an *Expanding* State of Grace through the mathematical precision of the Cycles of Inheritance.

| Date of Birth | | The Meeting of One's Living Teacher | Marriage Date | | The Divine-Marriage Anointing |

SEVEN-YEAR CYCLES OF GRACE-INHERITANCES

For a happy marriage, one must *earn* the respect of his or her mate on a 24-hour-a-day basis. So it is if one would earn the Divine-Marriage Anointing from the Spirit of God: he must prove worthy in the sight of God over the days, the months, the years.

Marriage with a physical mate begins with the speaking of *Vows*. A marriage is blessed by God as long as the husband and wife remain true to their wedding vows. Marriage or union with God also begins with vows or dedications spoken with love.

A husband and wife who worship God each day, keep His Commandments, and live within the Ethics of Jesus qualify for the receiving of *Marriage Grace-Inheritances*. Each Marriage Grace-Inheritance is received according to the same Law of Cycles that blesses the individual on the Path of Divine Union.

The moment a bride and groom speak their wedding vows,

they begin the Cycles leading to Marriage Grace-Inheritances. Over the years, as their loyalty and love are tested, they become the recipients of *Marriage Grace* through the Cycles of Inheritance. These Inheritances, as choice blessings from God, enable the couple to come closer together on all levels of their marriage: physical, emotional, mental and spiritual. Also, their marriage enables them to attain a finer Polarization of the masculine and feminine polarities within each of their own beings as individuals dedicated to God.

If wedding vows are not kept, the marriage begins a deterioration — and the Cycles of Marriage-Grace Inheritances are forfeited. The forfeiture of God's Blessings upon the marriage results in repetitive quarrels, frustrations, and often separation or divorce.

When two devotees of the higher life marry, their lives as individuals and as marital partners are doubly blessed by the Cycles of Inheritance. For example, if a man or a woman has served God faithfully in the single state, the Cycles of Inheritance began with the first prayer of dedication to God. If the devotee marries another spiritual aspirant one year later, their wedding vows begin the Cycles of Marriage-Grace Inheritances.

The Cycles of Grace-Inheritances are activated for each individual in his *personal* dedication to God and then again in his *joint-dedication* with a mate. In this, the marriage experiences increasing Grace-Inheritances, and the husband and wife, as individuals, also receive Grace-Inheritances. Such marriages blessed by God are *Grace-marriages*. The one and only key to the attaining of a Grace-marriage is: Faithfulness to one's wedding vows and the sanctification of the marriage through love for one another and love for God and His Commandments.

The activation of all key Cycles in one's life is God's Grace in action. God's Grace may occur as a single blessing or as showerings of blessings. The Grace of God is *cumulative* through the precise rhythm of the Cycles of Inheritance.

An earnest Truth-seeker is able to unite with the Bountifulness and Magnanimity of God through the diverse Cycles of Inheritance. To bask in the Light of God's Dimensional Grace is to become an enlightened seer in harmony with all Cycles occurring throughout the Universe — a Universe of Grace and Truth.

Man is not destined to be bestial or immoral. Man is destined to become a son of God, an heir of the Creator of all Stars and Galaxies. The Cycles of Inheritance will make it so.

The Spirit itself beareth witness with our spirit,
that we are the children of God: And if children,
then heirs; heirs of God, and joint-heirs with Christ.
—Romans 8:16,17

7

THE GLEAMING BRAIN

Undisciplined mind-strength is one's enemy.
Disciplined mind-strength is one's grace.
Disciplined mind-strength is one of the great
Rishi-virtues.

IN THE BEGINNING

Unto Adam also and to his wife did the Lord God
make coats of skins, and clothed them.
                    —Genesis 3:21

Man has never been an angel, and he has never been an animal. He is a specific creation under God.

Man possesses something of the animal nature in his primal nature; something of the angel nature in his soul nature. Therefore, he is harnessed in his own singularity between the instinctual primal and the heavenly niscient.

Before man as a soul took a coat of skin, his greatest activity was spent in absorption between these two kingdoms: the animal species kingdom and the angelic heavenly kingdom. His glandular system as yet inactive, he depended upon these two life-supporting virilities to build into him the subconscious part of his nature. In this subjective state, he was a triune-absorbing self. His body in this rare atmosphere of pre-gravity was the higher etheric body. Into this etheric body, he imprinted and recorded all that he heard and saw.

This period of man's existence before skin existence was totally God-subjective, similar to the time of the womb experience of present birth before movement. The mind of man in this time worked directly under and with the Archangels, the Devas, and the great Hierarchy or the Fathers.

The Earth in its beginning brought forth the rocks, the stones, the plants and the animals. The mineral atmospheres of these forms of life gave to the Earth a balance between the gases, the lavas and the rains. This produced a stabilization of currents between atmospheres in air, fire, earth, the planets and Earth.

When the Sun reached its equilibrium point to produce man's portions of Galaxy reciprocity, the etheric bodies of soul-man in their atom-charged energy processes took a leap into glandular function. In the present time, this may be likened to the first leap in the womb. Man-to-be as an ego, in bringing forth his glandular system, became a separate individual. Before this time, he had had a creative androgynity, being both male and female polarized within his developing and forming etheric body.

In the beginning, the two sides of the brain functioned toward God. After man took a coat of skin, the two sides of his brain functioned toward others, and particularly when male, toward female; and when female, toward male.

Man took on the glandular system and the coat of skin so that he might become an ego. From this time onward, man submerged the right side of his brain, which looked toward God, and used the left side of his brain, which was dominated by his glandular system.

Science desires to downgrade man into the animal

kingdom. There is no soul connection between the ape and man. Man is directly the progeny of our Father which art in Heaven and of the Hierarchy who are stationed at fixed-star constellations outside of this eternity system.

Our Father in this eternity system was never an ape or an angel—He is a Divine Being. We are made in His likeness and in the likeness of those who work with Him: Fathers of other eternity systems.

Man as a soul is a first-born in this Earth system. Man as an ego developing through Maya-mind Niscient power is a last-born—that is, the last to fulfill his being in this Earth system.

The forming mind of man and his God-Realization must come or return to the androgynous state. Using both the subjective right-side of the brain and the objective left side of the brain, he will receive in his own nature the meaning of his being in this Earth; he will be as Jesus, a hierarch or a god with the power to move mountains. Through his will and his visualization, he will master the Earth processes.

Man is an agent for God. His soul is at one with God. His hierarchy nature is seeking to inherit and use his own powers of hierarchy. Hierarchy nature begins with holiness, reverence, devotion toward God.

The heart, as a vortex for the emotional body, bears all of the burdens of the Undersoul. It is only through the heart's expanding love that one may begin to use his hierarchy nature, and thus transenergize the Undersoul into another brain. This brain of the future will give to man in his Kundalini system a fluidic-matrix power; he will use the will as a direct vehicle for God. This additional brain is overshadowing man's cortex system in the brain, that he may ultimately produce a gleaming brain or etheric brain.

In the etheric brain there is developing an *Omniscient Cell*, which will activate a third-cell function within every cell in the blood system. When man has blended the two hemispheres of his brain, his blood system will contain more of the volatile buoyancy of the ethers he lived in during the etheric state previous to the taking of the coat of skin. However, this ether will be a finer ether, whereby the atomic structure or atomic skeleton supporting the etheric body will be free as a comprehensible Cosmos-vehicle.

In the present-day, men use their atomic, etheric energy-body as a body between death and birth. This body exists after death in energy-fields similar to the neutrinos. The sensitivity of the neutrinos in the atomic world holds the key to man's understanding of gravity, anti-matter, and of creative processes of God. The units of measure in the neutrino fields of energy will lead man to discoveries far more important than his discoveries of the Moon and of his ventures into Galaxy-knowledge.

The neutrino point is the crossing-point into the Invisible Universe.

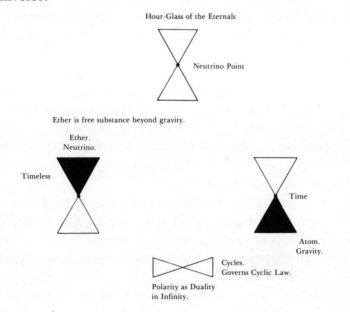

Hour-Glass of the Eternals

Neutrino Point

Ether is free substance beyond gravity.

Ether.
Neutrino.

Timeless

Time

Atom.
Gravity.

Cycles.
Governs Cyclic Law.

Polarity as Duality
in Infinity.

Water is the regulator of earth existence. Fire is the regulator of the atomic and molecular existence. Air is the regulator of the cell and sentient existence. Earth is the regulator of plant existence. Ether is the regulator of Time and Space, of Here and There, of Now and Then.

All Hierarchs have first-hand knowledge of ether. All must be accredited as Time and Space Initiates in the use of their hierarchy natures.

Time as potential in man is everlasting. Space as potential in man is limitlessness. Time and Space must be wed as energies supporting Eternal Spirit's intention in Creation.

Man is an androgynous soul-creation. His creature existence in Earth is a visitation to create and make the Earth-energies spiritual.

Every eternity system lives in cycles as to timing. An eternity system can be young as a child can be young. An eternity system can become a full and mature eternity system.

In the cyclic periods of birth and death to an eternity system, the system undergoes a number of endings or black-hole experiences whereby it draws into itself all it has sent forth. These are called the Dark-Aeon, Master or Grand Kali-Yuga times. Every black hole experienced in a galaxy is a time of rest for the energy processes to return to their original beginnings. This is accomplished in the state of a seeming passivity.

The positive principle of Creation is the going forth on a charted sea willed in God. The respite stages are restorative, similar to man's need to sleep.

The Time-system of the Universe as related to Cosmos and to all forming things, inclusive of man and of worlds, undergoes sleep or death, rest or restoration, birth or creation. All are part of *Time* on Cosmos scales as to units of measure in the Will of God.

Every black hole transenergizes itself at the ending of its

rest into a white hole, whereby the polarity atom-point in an eternity system sounds the Tone of another Day.

Death and life and birth—these three belong to God, to His Creation, to Man, and to all things He has created. These are ever existing.

Time and Space are husband and wife. Mind and super-mind are husband and wife. All is polarized as yin and yang, or feminine and masculine.

Awareness and consciousness provide man with the key to his own mystery. His consciousness is both Cosmic and Cosmos. It is all inside of his soul-nature.

In the building of an eternity system, as a will-agent for God, one demotes himself into the primal. The vibrational limitation in his primal nature, working with his soul nature, has both awakening and forgetting capacity. The more primal and instinctual, the more man forgets his Godly origins. He fails to remember that he has sealed into him within the ordered patterns of the Eternals the orders to take him on the Path from star to star. It is Provident that he must forget his creative hierarchy origins so that he may master by direct absorption each atmosphere, and thereby vitalize it with sentience.

All is energy. Everything in man is energized through the star-routes and the planets. What he calls his ego is a prize gift enabling him to build for God.

Spiritual Man says: "In the beginning there *is* God." Primal and ego man says: "In the beginning there *was* God."

MEDITATION AND THE CONSTANT OF GOD

God is the Constant in Total Universe.

God's Love is a Constant. When one is constant, he is in God. When meditating, one must make union with his Constant, which is the Constant of God in him. He must make

FOUR DIFFERENT ZODIAC INFLUENCES
UPON HUMAN CONSCIOUSNESS

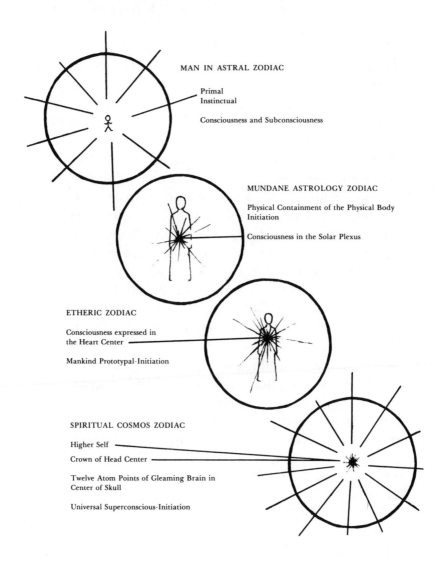

MAN IN ASTRAL ZODIAC

Primal
Instinctual

Consciousness and Subconsciousness

MUNDANE ASTROLOGY ZODIAC

Physical Containment of the Physical Body
Initiation

Consciousness in the Solar Plexus

ETHERIC ZODIAC

Consciousness expressed in
the Heart Center

Mankind Prototypal-Initiation

SPIRITUAL COSMOS ZODIAC

Higher Self

Crown of Head Center

Twelve Atom Points of Gleaming Brain in
Center of Skull

Universal Superconscious-Initiation

the effort in his physical life to be in touch with his Constant at all times.

Extended polarity permits man of the Earth to live in only one side of polarity at a time. If he is wholly engrossed in physical concerns, it is impossible for him to know anything of the heavenly. An extended polarity keeps one in a state of total engrossment in whatever world he finds himself.

The work to produce a more centered polarity state and to be in touch with one's Constant is a battle of forces, of energies, of will. The more one yearns to know God, the more his extended polarity relaxes and comes closer to a balanced sense of reality in both Heaven and in Earth.

To know something of dying and its meaning, one must be at one with his Constant, which is the Constant of God in him. His Constant assures him of God.

Freeing the Constant is the work. Living in both worlds is the potential. All must strive to be in their Constant.

The Constant is the hierarchy nature; it is never changing. The Constant is the Divine Primordial, having the power to project from Itself the Likeness of God and the Image of Hierarchy.

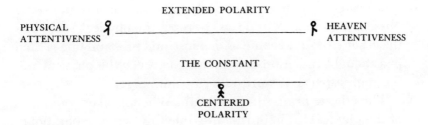

Man is as he is because there is a Constant in every thing created of God. Maya determines that man is in a state of changing. Holy Spirit works to bring relief from Maya.

The Constant of God in man is his own Divinity in God. This is the Infinity in the finite. The Infinity in man is the soul; the finite in man is the world, the body. Esse or movement is the freeing agent maintaining the Constant or the Infinite within.

Radiance is a giving-maintenance of the Constant. Radiation from radiance is the state of Dharma in the act of Passing. One radiates energy or light from the Constant's use of supernatural energy in the soul. A radiating energy is the healing presence of the Constant.

The Triad Preparation for Meditation is: Attention, Concentration, Contemplation. Meditation without these is limited; with these, Meditation is limitless.

In the average person, the etheric brain is working so fast that it is not in contact with the physical brain except in rare instances in dream life when one may have a brief glimpse of the thought-velocity in the etheric brain.

When one begins intensive initiation, he encounters the etheric brain in his consciousness level—and the result is overwhelming energy-thought acceleration. His work as an initiate is to unite the etheric brain with the physical brain.

All persons opening the etheric-brain process begin with accelerated thinking. This causes intense pressure upon the physical brain motor-reflexes. In time, the physical brain and the etheric brain become as one instrument—and one is then in a thought radiation coordinating between the physical and the high aspects of spirituality in thinking.

The etheric brain survives death. When it takes command of the physical brain during life, one thinks in the parabolic-chain action of soul-memory. Thus, he can do miraculous things through the expansion of consciousness.

Meditation enables the two brain functions to accelerate. One who meditates may be compared to a woman who gives birth to a child without pain.

For those who have little or no religiosity, a psychic-energy membrane keeps separated the two hemispheres of the brain; this creates traumatic and psychiatric phenomena due to inflation of the ego. This is a psychic state, a non-spiritual state. Therefore, men today who have no religiosity are undergoing psychic hysterias and derangement.

In the use of alcohol and drugs, the two hemispheres of the brain widen, moving farther apart from one another. One loses his coordination with his physical adaptations, with his etheric, emotional and mental.

The left side of the brain is Yang. The right side of the brain is Yin. The Yin and Yang currents in the breath cross at the eyebrow center; the great cranial nerves cross over. Yang becomes Yin, and Yin becomes Yang within the two hemispheres of the brain.

Logic active in the left side of the brain produces Mathematics, Music, and use of the senses to explore the physical world. One has spiritualized Induction and Intuition on the right side of the brain.

The left side of the brain is the materialistic side. This side of the brain takes care of keeping one alive in the physical world, supporting his physical needs. The right side of the brain, when functioning with *balance*, keeps one functioning within the realities of his soul and the Spiritual Worlds.

When one starts meditating, the ethers in the two hemispheres of the brain come closer together until finally they interlink as the Great Dome. Then all mental attributes and spiritual faculties unite *equally*, making a person a whole being. Every meditation is seeking to make this fusion a reality. When this occurs, the Omniscient Cell functions; man becomes a greater dimensional being while living in the Earth; his mind is as the Jesus Mind.

The crown of the head is the apex point corresponding to the Galaxy Gate. When the Yin and Yang hemispheres of the

etheric brain interlace, Buddhi becomes active; one is no
longer fixed to the duality eternity-system relativities. He is
Galaxy-related. Buddhi will interpret to him what exists in
his own Galaxy nature.

The *Galaxy Consciousness* begins at the point of the Higher
Self and goes to the point between the eyebrows. Between the
Higher Self and the eyebrow center are millions of atoms in
direct communication with the Galaxy Fatherhood of our
eternity system and of our eternal origins. When one is in
communion with the Galaxy Atoms pouring down from the
Higher Self, he is at one with the Total Universe.

The uncreated is always trying to become the created.
When one reaches the Galaxy Atoms, he is in the Transcendent. The Eternal Sustaining Atom centered in the Higher
Self is like a great generating system where the holy inter-
connection is made between man and God.

> *The* mudra posture *of the interlaced fingers with
> the thumbs not touching, but in very close prox-
> imity to each other, automatically moves the two
> hemispheres of the etheric brain in an arch
> meeting-place whereby they are interlaced. One is
> then in a state of Transcendence within Buddhi.*

THE COAXING SPIRIT AND JEHOVAH

> *A* Mantra *is a portion of the Word. A* Yantra *is
> a method through which one is initiated through
> symbolic, myth consciousness. A* Yantra *is accom-
> panied by charts and diagrams proving interrela-
> tionships between soul, mind and action. The Yan-
> tra technique opens the soul-record of the Earth
> and of the individual.*

The left side of the brain is the Jehovah side. The right side
of the brain is the mystic side. The etheric canal between

these two is now closing in the fusion between the Jehovah thought-compulsions and the mystic interior intuitions. The Gleaming Brain will function, and the Christ Mind will be free; this is a physiological as well as spiritual event of great importance for each one in the Earth.

Total erasement of sins occurs through the right hemisphere of the brain during cyclic mastery as to Memory and Time. The more one has true meditation and opens the high side of Yantra, the more the Time-mastery within the right hemisphere of the brain will erase and devour all memories containing sin and sinning.

Forgiveness functions through this Grace-of-God provision within the right hemisphere of the brain. When this occurs, one is as newborn as a babe and as a bride with the Bridegroom.

The dark side of Jehovah contains a coaxing and condemning spirit. The tester presents himself as the coaxer or tempter and then condemns him whom he has coaxed, and records the sinning as an obstacle to be met and to be mastered.

In the Jehovah side of the brain, there are three cyclic flows of Time: the tamasic, the rajasic and the sattvic. When one unites with the sattvic, he is then ready to receive the power to erase evil and non-grace actions and memories.

When one has continuous access to the sattvic flow of Time in the Jehovah side of the brain, he is free of the Time-units of measure. His cycles of Cause and Effect become God-Realized through blessed events of healing and teaching.

The initiate has the power to erase his sin-records through meditation during the higher Yantra initiatory periods. The coaxing spirit is restrained in its subtle, suggestible functioning in the life of one who has reached the higher Yantra-knowing.

Satan walks in the garden of the left hemisphere of the brain. He is the tester and the coaxing spirit leading man into temptation.

In all wars, plagues, famines, Satan is present. And more than any, he is present when one is ready or ripe to enter the Path. All who enter into the Path of Self-Denial through Jesus must encounter the coaxing wiles of the adversary.

In this time, there is a super-heating condition in the base of the skull where the Rudra powers through Yantra-mastery must free the right hemisphere of the brain and unite the interflow between the two hemispheres of brain and consciousness functioning.

All religions of secular nature, where there are ecclesiastical political situations, are expressing the left hemisphere or Jehovah side of the brain. The outer religious formats do not communicate with the right hemisphere processes of illumination.

When one has become saturated with ecclesiastical political systems in religion, he is ready for the trials within the marriage between the two areas of the brain. Religiosity in one's nature determines that he will undergo the hemisphere-trials that he may expand etherically the brain functions into higher degrees of soul-expression.

For many lives, one can remain at the Yantra Station and undergo all the initiatory variations from life to life so that he may gain the true garment of androgynity in Christ.

There are many fragmented systems of occult and psychic expression in the world. It is rare and unusual when any of these speak of the Christ or understand Jesus as He is.

Fragmented gurus are ego-inflated, aggrandizing their podiums or their sitting position. By this do we know them, that he who is separate is also on the coaxing-path of the dark.

Where the Christ is not lived, spoken of and understood, where Jesus is deleted and watered-down suitable to personality and psychological interpretation, the coaxing spirit within the dark side of Jehovah is expressed.

Satan is the dark side of Jehovah. The dark side of Jehovah, which does not accept the Christ, produces the material mind, the materialistic life and the materialistic predominance in human relationships.

One has his own Time-machine against sin and sinning. This exists in the right hemisphere of the brain.

On the level of sin in Jehovah, one is subjected to prolonged timing of sins and their correction. Under the Christ functioning in the right side of the brain, one acts within the mastery of Time with the competency to erase and devour sins and the memory of sins, and thus be free and liberated, timeless through soul-powers within the Christ.

The Crown of the Head is the Center for the Christ. Between the eyebrows is the corridor where the Love of Jesus flows upward toward the Christ.

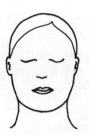

The *Virgin* is active in the right side of the back of the brain. Mary works to give one Chastity so that he can receive the Immaculate Conception in the heart.

John the Baptist works through the *Rudra* or left side of the brain stem. John the Baptist works to give one the Power of the Holy Spirit whereby one has purification and morality. This is the *Yantra* center.

The John-the-Baptist Power cannot work without the Virgin. It is only through the Chastity Immaculate Conception that the Birth of Jesus can come so that the Christ may embody Himself in the world.

Set me free, O most Holy Chastity.
　All things are pure to the pure.
Most Holy Chastity, be with me.
Most Holy Chastity, set me free in body, in love,
　in mind.
Most Holy Chastity, be with me.
Most Holy Chastity, watch with me.
Most Holy Chastity, keep me to principle true.
Anoint me, Most Holy Chastity, that I may will
　in the Will and be free.
Most Holy Chastity, fly into my bosom and set me
　free, that I may soar in the bosom of God, in
　His Holy Chastity, and see all things in the most
　pure light circulating, creating, within the
　Uncreate in both day and night.

THE VISIBLE AND INVISIBLE SUN

Where color is, there is God's Presence as light.

The central Cord in the Spine, or Sushumna, is the Cord of the Constant, producing Virtue. The Sushumna Cord in the spine builds the will power of man. The matrix of the will in the spine is ruled by the Sun.

At the first rising of the Sun, the Invisible Sun and the physical Sun unite at the kidney point where reside the adrenal glands. At the moment of the first touch of the rising Sun, the Sushumna cord in the spine quickens the will to live and the will to survive. Through this function of the ignited Sushumna, one retains the memory of the night experience. Accompanying this is the conscience-ethic provided directly by the Soul, that man may do the works of the day within the spirit of rightness according to the Blueprint of God and His Law. The more one has awareness of this union between Sushumna and the rising Sun, the more stabilized his actions and motives for the day.

Man sleeps at night in the cradle of the Invisible Sun. The physical Sun in his nature, carried over from the day, supports his sleep, that he may awaken to another day of work and creation.

The Sun manufactures the color in all living things, supporting vision and visualization. The Sun leaves its mark of color on the flower, on the plant, on the sky. Wherever vision is, light and color, products of the Sun, record the message of God as Light.

In the night's sleep, man is exposed to the visible Sun and Invisible Sun. The physical Sun supports the daytime memory. The Invisible Sun provides the soul-memory for the night's experience in sleep.

Every man witnesses the memory of God as Light expressed through the Sun. He sees in the flower the color of the memory of the Sun.

Even though many Suns go down upon the flower — and the night of darkness falls — the flower retains its color. So does man experience the Light of God through his own soul-coloring.

In all states of consciousness, the memory of God supports the function of mind, will, survival, memory, conscience. In the night's sleep, the soul colors the experiences of the night, and indents them in the growing, extending soul-faculties for the mind.

Each day one must enter into the Invisible Sun within and receive the reviving influence of its rising. Each day he must reproduce the Invisible-Sun coloring made visible through the actions and thinking of the day.

The Gleaming Brain more freely functions in the night's sleep. It is a product of the Invisible Sun. As man develops the Gleaming Brain through meditative procedures and night-memory, he will extend his senses into capacities unknown, brilliant beyond the thought-processes of the present time.

The rising Sun starts at approximately 3:00 A.M. This affects the spine and the adrenal glands, the nervous system of the spine supporting the brain for the physical acts of the day. Before men technically record the rising of the physical Sun, the electricities from both the physical Sun and the Invisible Sun are active in the Earth.

Man arises each day with charged, vital, life-force energies. Should one fail to have a response to these life-giving energy processes, he has in some way lost the will to act and to live in the physical world. This can occur in sickness or in the psychic mental processes of the emotions. One who arises in the morning desiring to die is committing suicide on the psychic level. Those who prepare for a sacred death awaken in this time with the sweet retention of grace-memories of life and a strong desire to leave in the Earth the imprints of their love and fidelity.

As one ages, sleep impresses him with all of the variables of mind development and body encounter. The older one grows, the more spiritualized are his dreams if he has lived for others, has believed in God, and has run the course of his life with ethic.

Dream mastery is as important as waking mastery. Both are necessary to one another for soul and mind survival.

THE ADRENAL GLANDS

The Gleaming Brain becomes permanent when the lower impulses are purified. They are purified when one decides to accept the disciplines of the spiritual life.

Polarization is made in the brain; it begins in the adrenal glands. The will-power center is expressed through the adrenal glands working at the kidney level. The will-power

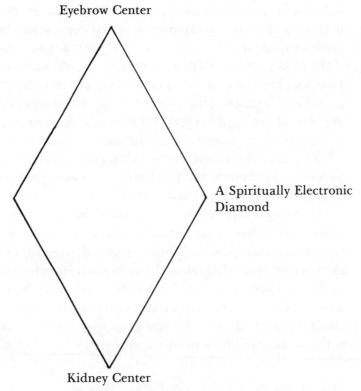

Eyebrow Center

A Spiritually Electronic
Diamond

Kidney Center

matrix as a vehicle for survival is seated in the adrenal-glands station. The primal and primordial compulsions of the will, acting as yin and yang polarities in the various bodies, reside at this adrenal-glands station.

When the passions are amoral, the will center at the yin-yang point adjacent to the adrenal glands sends the sexual currents toward the sacral energies. Lust is maintained, and the upper brain or most essential brain is short-circuited from the holier energies given off by the soul. The lowest chakra becomes inflamed sensuously; thoughts are always centered upon sex and sex partners and consummation of sex.

One yoga posture which prevents this lust-activity is the reverse posture of standing on the head. One having problems with lust-intrusions in his thoughts should use at least once or twice a day the inverted postures of yoga with the head downward and the feet upward. This posture opens the base of the brain center, drawing upward the yin and yang currents into the essential or upper brain. The reverse postures should not be maintained longer than fifteen seconds each. One should not do these postures if he has high blood pressure or any tendency toward heart disease.

When one encounters the hardship laws, this is due to misdirected sexual energies. The hardship laws expose a person to the lower devachan dual-devas.

The lust-pressure sensualities expose one to the grotesque levels of devachan. Any form of creation stemming from the grotesque level produces the distorted side of creation. Children conceived by those living within the grotesque are lustful in their own lives of the future — and their mind-energies are very often retarded or creating some form of disease of the body and the limbs, such as a spastic condition in the muscular portions of the body.

THE PITUITARY GLAND AND PINEAL GLAND

One of the seeming cyclic mysteries is that man is regulated to a certain height due to the work between the pituitary gland and gravity. In some planetary systems, men are giants and some are extremely small — all due to the gravity playing upon the glandular system. In an eternity system, the overall *height* of man determines the mental-body function.

Moon plus gravity builds man's internal system or organism. The Sun plus gravity builds the exterior system. The planetary forces adjacent to the central system, or Earth, assist the Moon and the Sun in the building of the structure of man.

Three other planets will join this eternity system. Our Sun

will then act fully within the Thirteenth Principle of the Christ. At the present time, this Earth System having but nine planets functions through the nine openings of the body. When the three planets join this eternity system, consciousness will function through thirteen energies. When these planets enter into the etheric sphere or the world-soul atom, two will come together — and a third planet will follow after a long interval. When this occurs, this eternity system will have fulfilled itself.

The Earth awaits the coming to birth of these three additional planets. The mind of man as a vehicle of consciousness will be in a hierarchy state with the additional energies pouring into his brain and spinal column.

The present brain of man is controlled by the Moon. The advanced ego has both the Sun and the Moon influencing his brain. Only through Archetypal Instruction does an Initiate open the Gleaming Brain which is fed by the Sun.

The pineal gland in man acts as the matrix for the Sun energy. The pituitary gland acts as the matrix for the Moon and the Lunar energies.

Since the coming of the Christ, the Indestructible Atom in the center of the forehead has placed extreme pressure on both the pineal and pituitary glands. This has created extensions of self-aggression in mankind at large. This also has extended the Genesis stages in evolvement. The present Self-Genesis coming to birth in mankind is creating disunion rather than union.

Each planet, when added to the present nine, will bring its own moon or moons. These moons will directly change the axis and rotational, orbital function of the Sun and the planets.

The Omniscient Cell in the brain is the Jesus Cell. Men will be ultimately *like Jesus*. They will walk on water; they will appear and disappear. They will command the force nature of this Earth System. They will think through hierarch units of measure through the Gleaming Brain.

This Earth is now in its adolescence. It is suffering the growing pains of ignorance. Man as an inhabitant of this Earth is yet immature. He suffers growing pains with the Earth. The sum total of his sins is due to ignorance, to unknowing. The religion of the Self-Genesis man is to know and to act through the Christ Spirit.

Through the Open Door of Galaxy, men now receive a new lease, a new contract with the Landlord of the Universe. (God is our Lessor and we are the lessees.) We are given Time in units of measure, in periodic cycles, that we may remain in balance. The greatest miracle of all is that man, since the Christ took command of this eternity system, is a conscious partaker and participant in Universal Creation.

UNITS OF MEASURE AND TIME

> *The Lord shall preserve thy going out and thy coming in from this time forth, and even for evermore.*
>
> *—Psalm 121:8*

All Time is energy. Energy as Time is experienced in units of measure.

Every plane has its own system of timing. There is an etheric scale of timing, an astral scale of timing, a mental scale of timing, and a spiritual scale of Timelessness. One must have equal measures of Time in each of these planes before he can move beyond phenomena or relativity into Timelessness.

One earns the units of measure of Time in each plane through initiation in the physical world. The gravity clock of Time in the physical plane is the most difficult to master, as man in physical life is sealed away from direct knowledge of the supernatural laws and eternal laws supporting the units of Time in Creation.

Man on the physical plane exists in the self-hypnosis of self-preservation and survival. Therefore, in his outer consciousness, he has only conceptual knowledge of Time and the units of measure in life through his dependence upon his senses or sensory antennas.

While living in the physical world, man is constantly aware of the danger of death, failing to understand the units of measure in the energy-processes of Time and Space. Knowing only his limited lesser self and its awkwardness, he restricts himself to centralized spheres of industry, thinking this to be the Real.

When one meditates upon the Universals, he understands and lives within the four planes housing his consciousness life and the four bodies housing his soul. In the discovering nature of meditation, he steps out of Time and Space into Universal Creation.

Prophecy is a function of the Gleaming Brain. When one has the Gift of Prophecy, he has overcome the Time-barrier existing within the system of Maya and the system of Karma. Sanat Kumara, or the Ancient of Days, is the Initiator for Time-freeing, whereby one is freed from the Maya fixity or limited units of measure.

SPACE AND TIMING

Spiritual diligence is the use of Time through persevering in practices and in dedication.

People who want something without earning are offending one of the greatest laws of Timing. Those who take something without earning it, must multiply it back to God through servitude to some unpleasant task, situation or condition through which they clean up the offense of debts against Timing.

Inflated increase without rightful purchase through the sweat of right work and effort is similar to a toadstool which looks to the eye to be rightful for nourishment, yet is filled with death-poisons or substances. Wrongful claim to things, possessions, love, place, honor — all are lethal in their poisons and destroying.

When one heals someone else or himself, he has fulfilled a law in Timing. He thus becomes a user of Space; he uses the energy he has drawn forth with his healing power. His enlargement is larger than encasement, and his expansion powers are expanded. He becomes another person by the very fact that he is living in extended Space through expansion of consciousness. He becomes *another* rather than the old. He puts off the old man. He must learn to live with the new man.

That which is in the Time-Sphere having an ending is within the Time-Cycles, but that which is in the ending of a Time-Cycle is Space within the Cycle of Time which gives new birth and a beginning. This is the Controlling Movement Element in the Spirit of God; for all things that end have within them Space-energies which ascertain without variation that in every ending there is a birth to the new.

He who meditates builds accumulative Space: Space for consciousness on the level of self as self-awareness. Mastery of Space through meditation uses every second and moment of energy in the Time-Cycles, that Space may be his habitation while living in an enclosure.

When an eternity system ends, the Space it has collected during its interim or eras becomes the vortex-field for the utilization of Time-energy, and a higher degree of Space-mastery takes control of the Earth System. Thus, Solar Systems are born and die and are born again. This is Reincarnation on the grandest scale, which only Spirit can measure and equate, for what Spirit measures determines all beginnings, their purpose, their plan.

An initiate must master his Timing, and be ever alert to his Timing as a point where he will fulfill the Plan of God for the world and all worlds.

Everyone has a *race-matrix* that determines his units of measure for physical life. If he has earned through his soul a *grace-matrix*, he extends his life length of years beyond his seventies. His longevity grace-matrix years are years of wisdom, intelligible Passing. His sage-like knowledge is sought after and longed for by those near and far.

The last fruit on the tree in the ending of the season is the sweetest, and the budding flower on the tree is the prettiest. And the lotus in the last budding is the most beautiful in its centering and its fragrance. So are the latter years of matrix-grace giving longevity.

All teachers having left their mark have lived to be aged. Jesus left the world in His 33rd year: His age was of the Cosmos; His longevity, of the Universal. Jesus was ageless from birth to Crucifixion. He was Master of Time, Place and Space.

TIME-ERASEMENT

> *Grace for grace and grace within Grace come*
> *with the reincarnation pattern and design.*

One who manipulates is distorting Time. When a leap is made in evolvement through Marking and Tracing, Constancy and Attentiveness, one erases Time which has been offended through deviation.

Time is offended through lust, hate, greed, separateness, envy and doubt. Each of these, when overcome, removes the necessity in karma.

Heavily-laden karma is time-consuming as to extension of years on the Wheel of Karma. To come into timing with one's Grace is to truly know one's own face or soul-countenance reflecting the Constant of God.

Time is equated as a functional Grace-vehicle. Through Grace, one who comes into timing receives gifts, joys. The most happy days are the days spent in seconds, moments and hours within the Coinciding Principle where everything is proving the Law of God as just, right, perfect.

The greatest gift of all for having fulfilled Timing is the opportunity to sit at the feet of instruction; to serve God, that others may be enlightened; and to heal the unknowing of the spiritually ignorant. This is the perfect testimony that one is in timing to the voice of the Holy Spirit speaking from the soul. When one finds himself at the feet of instruction — providing the way of karmic obliteration that he may serve God out of the fullness of his heart — he has received the true marking in his forehead that he *is* in the Will of God. For he who acts ethically within Timing is within the Will of God.

Until one places his will in God, he must suffer the sharp, swordlike spokes of the Wheel of Karma and be shredded through ego-demotion. To give enlightenment to others is to take hold of one's own Time and to directly influence the timing of others through the grace of the Coinciding Principle.

THE COVENANT OF PUNCTUALITY

When one is in timing, he has access to the Gleaming Brain. He is a prophet for the Universals, and he has achieved to some degree at-one-ment with the Spirit of God through Space.

Lack of punctuality and being out of timing in the Grand Scheme of the present and the Grand Plan of the Cosmos, produces self-hatred and opens one to irritability from others.

Being *out of things* makes one an outcast. On the fringe, he cannot enter into the Activity Principle in control of the Universe. He is suffered by his companions as being out of things, as being a nuisance, as being selfish — and he is considered lazy, tamasic.

A non-punctual person rarely keeps his word. He is forced by the law to keep his word painfully; and if he is awakening to the need for punctuality, he is embarrassed by his exploitation of Time.

Punctuality and attentiveness are companions. One who is always late has misdirected attentiveness produced by scatteredness in thought and feeling.

All unpunctual persons have more astral nature than mental-body nature. To come into timing through the Covenant of Punctuality produces mind-strength, will-power and mental-body perfection.

Keeping one's word and being on time are equal in virtue. In keeping the discipline of Punctuality, one not only has the virtue of being in union with the Cosmos, but he is also united with his own conscience. He receives, without any form of deviation, the Guiding Principle in all of his affairs.

One must realize that to be punctual requires on his part to be patient with those who are chronically unpunctual. Through patience, he gains the virtue of healing. He should never permit the deviation of others as to promises, vows or timing to influence him in any degree, or else he becomes the victim of his own irritability — and he will find himself sitting in judgment of the conduct of others.

It must be remembered that Punctuality has a companion virtue, which is Patience. On observing Punctuality as fully as possible, one will find that his prayers and the timing of his grace will become an ever-present reality in his life. But he should also be patient with the Correcting Principle which accompanies the practice of Punctuality.

If one has been tamasic in keeping his appointments, his promises or work-status as to timing, he will come to see his own past deviation in its true light, and thus step out of the vibrations of *existing* rather than *living*. To be punctual is to be filled with enthusiasm, ever-ready for a new adventure, which can be experienced only in the spiritual veracities of Cosmos and Cosmic Law.

The punctual person rises with the Sun. The unpunctual person is irritated by the morning's sunrise, resenting its reminder that the day is given for creation.

HIERARCHY INHERITANCE

The Sun is the energy used by Hierarchy to stabilize the chromosomes and balance them. Hierarchy works with the chromosomes. The planets, the Moon and the Angels work with the genes.

The lowest matrix, which extends from the feet to the pelvic center, is connected with the Moon. The middle matrix, centered between the pelvic center and the heart, is connected with the Sun. The energy-currents of the highest matrix begin in the heart and move upward to the crown of the head; this matrix works directly with the Gleaming Brain. The spiritualized person cultivates and develops the third-matrix extension through the mind.

The involuntary nature of man is a gift of God. The involuntary system is directly connected with the Law of Increase in God. The third matrix determines how the true self-nature evolves. There can be no reality of self until one relates to the spiritual through and of and by himself.

Until the coming of Christ through Jesus, man lived totally within the involuntary system. With the Passion of Jesus, and the opening of the Indestructible Atom, man began to create himself. Consequently, all sins of mankind caused by offense against the chromosome system and the gene system must be mastered by the infinite processes of unfoldment through the self.

The ten fingers relate to Hierarchy. The distribution of the Dharma is: Giving and Serving. The hands and the ten fingers are the symbols of the Great Law or the Dharma. The nervous system in the palm of the hand works directly with the Gleaming Brain. The palm of the hand is one of the great centers of the Eternals.

The Maha-Mudra system pertains to posture of the hand. Behind the symbol of the posture of the hand are the Great Laws.

The hands closed into a tight fist are as a closed bud of a lotus or the unmanifested Dharma. The open hand facing the one blessed is the symbol of blessing, giving, serving, healing.

INHERITANCE AND SUCCESSION

The highest point of Inheritance is *Succession*: one Teacher passing his mantle to another. As Saint Paul said, "I planted, Apollos watered" (1 Corinthians 3:6); and as Elijah passed his mantle to Elisha, so is the true Inheritance which is inevitable as an heir of God. The real Inheritance is what one inherits from the Teacher.

Jesus and the Father gave man Heaven as a whole Inheritance. The Teacher gives to one the toll-fare and the toll-way by which one finds and inhabits the Inheritance.

One is led by his Teacher into brief initiatory excursions whereby he receives a glimpse of divine-energy functioning in precision and perfection. If the disciple is co-atom to his Teacher, he is preparing for the day when he also will become a guide to celestial realities.

Every true Teacher must set up an enterprise in the life of his disciple, always recognizing that Succession is a great Law, and that what he passes to his disciple is a reverent repository of grace, truth and wisdom.

Siddhi powers or gifts, when given by a teacher devoid of devotion, dedication and foresight, become hindrances harming rather than blessing. The true Passer gives that which fits the one receiving. To give to a disciple a gift not suitable to his range and capacity offends the Law of Succession.

The Great Immortals gave to man the Universal Truths. Man, as a protege and eventually an initiate, comes under the tutelage of the Great Immortals who are the tutelary-deities for mind as consciousness.

The process of opening the Gleaming Brain uses Time and Space, Memory and Conscience; the Inner Eye is opened, and man sees as a seer and a knower or a Nisciene within the superconscious light of the soul.

... Jonathan Murro

8

TIME-POLARIZATION

Time was created as an image of eternity.
—Plato, 427–347 B.C.

The world was created with time and not in time.
—St. Augustine of Hippo, 6th Century

Let time flow by, with which we flow on to be transformed into the glory of the children of God.
—St. Francis of Sales (1567–1622)

THE SIX

And God saw everything that he had made, and behold, it was very good. And the evening and the morning were the sixth day.
—Genesis 1:31

• The Old Testament describes God's creation of the heavens and the Earth in 6 Great Days.

- The 6 is the number of God's *Law*. The Law of God is creating the Earth, the Solar System, Man, the Universe.

- The speed of light is 6 trillion miles a year.

- The average distance between Stars in our part of the Milky Way Galaxy is 6 light-years.

- The planet Earth travels 66,600 miles an hour in its orbit around the Sun.

- The Earth weighs 6 billion trillion tons.

- The surface of the Sun, the Photosphere, is 6000° C.

- The second layer of the Sun, the Convection Zone, is 60,000 miles thick.

- Sunspots are usually 6,000 miles wide.

- Saturn is the 6th planet from the Sun.

- Saturday, or Saturn's Day, is the 6th day of the week.

- The symbol of the planet Saturn is the scythe, symbolizing Father Time.

- *Time* is based on the Law of Cycles related to the 6: 60 seconds in a minute; 60 minutes in an hour; 24 (2 + 4 = 6) hours in a day; 24 (2 + 4 = 6) Time Zones in the planet Earth.

- The ancient Chinese considered the 6 to be the number of the Universe.

- The Yin and Yang symbol 69 represents the blending between the Feminine and the Masculine; Fertility; Polarization.

• Saint Martin called the 6 an "eternal law."

• An atom of carbon consists of 6 electrons circling a nucleus of 6 protons and 6 neutrons. From carbon comes the diamond. In the spiritual life of an individual, the carbon symbolizes his initiatory lessons and transformations through which he attains the diamond — the symbol of *Illumination*.

• Snowflakes are 6-pointed creations with multitudinous variations of geometrical beauty and grace.

• The cells in a beehive are 6-sided engineering master-pieces.

• The hexagon-energies of the 6 ⬡ , when used for evil or unholy purposes, create a *hex* or curse.

• The early Christians believed the 6 to be the number of sin. The failure to fulfill God's Laws (6) creates a sin or self-curse.

• In the Science of *Declension* (Ann Ree Colton), the 6 represents Sex, Healing and Service.

• All dedicated healers work through the healing energies of the number 6. The process of Polarization represented by the 6 heals the ills and woes caused by inharmonious polarities. Where there is imbalance in the Polarities, there is discord, unhappiness, sorrow; where there is polarization, there is healing, harmony, happiness, fulfillment.

• The vowel "O" correlates to the number 6. The holy words *GOD* and *OM* contain the concealed power of the 6 as the lone vowel.

• The Kundalini-energy flowing downward follows the pattern of the ⟨ 6; such persons express their lower natures through lust, greed, pride, materiality and sensuality. When the Kundalini-energy is reversed through spiritual practices and worship-dedications, the heart and the mind become enlightened instruments of service to God. ⟨ 6 In this, the Kundalini energies are moving upward toward the Jewel in the Lotus Chakra over the Crown of the Head, thereby producing the Spiritual Gifts of Healing, Prophecy and Revelation.

• The ancient Hindu symbol for the Heart Chakra (Anahata) is the 6-pointed Star.

• The major symbol of the Hebrew faith is the 6-pointed Star.

• The 6-pointed Star, as a Universal symbol, symbolizes the *Marriage* or *Polarization* between Time and Space, the Feminine and the Masculine, the individual and God, Heaven and Earth.

• *Solomon's Seal* is the 6-pointed star with black and white interlaced triangles. The white triangle signifies the light of God in the state of Manifestation; the dark triangle, the Unmanifest.

• The Book of Revelation in the New Testament reveals the importance of the number 666. *"Here is wisdom. Let him that hath understanding count the number of the beast: for it is the number of a man; and his number is Six hundred threescore and six." (Revelation 13:18)*

• Virgo, the Virgin, is the 6th Constellation-House in the zodiac.

• During the 6th month of Elizabeth's pregnancy with the babe who would become John the Baptist, the Archangel Gabriel announced to Mary the birth of her Son, Jesus. *"And in the sixth month the angel Gabriel was sent from God unto a city of Galilee named Nazareth, To a virgin espoused to a man whose name was Joseph, of the house of David; and the virgin's name was Mary." (St. Luke 1:26,27)*

• Each Seraphim Angel has 6 wings. (Isaiah 6:1-3) *"The six wings of the Seraphim provide the six wisdom-nourishments regarding worship of God." (Ann Ree Colton)*

• The Crucifixion of Jesus began in the 6th hour. *"Now from the sixth hour there was darkness over all the land unto the ninth hour." (St. Matthew 27:45)*

• The three Master Numbers are: 11, physical mastery; 22, spiritual mastery; 33, higher initiate. Jesus experienced His Resurrection and Ascension in His 33rd year (3 + 3 = 6).

PURIFICATION AND POLARIZATION

And every man that hath this hope in Him purifieth himself even as He is pure.

—1 John 3:3

Polarization is a great Principle of the Universe. All creations in God's Plan are either polarized or are seeking to become polarized. Man is striving to become a polarized being in harmony with Universal Polarization and Creation.

The polarization necessary for Spiritual Illumination is attained through purification. The purifying processes of the spiritual life are constantly working to refine, stabilize and harmonize the various polarities within one's being.

"God is a Spirit: and they that worship him must worship him in spirit and in truth." (St. John 4:24). Jesus, a Polarized Being, emphasized the importance of worship. Enlightened Teachers of every faith stress the necessity of daily worship through one or more expressions of devotion to God. Meditation, Prayer, Fasting, Almsgiving, and other worship-disciplines produce miracles of healing within oneself because of the Polarization that occurs through reverent worship.

Whenever one worships God, he lifts his senses and their awareness of Earth-Time toward the Soul and its Eternal Polarization in Cosmos. The Soul, in turn, unites him with the polarity-energies of the Sun, the Moon and the Planets. Thus, during reverent worship, one becomes receptive to mighty energies that produce increasing polarizations in all areas of his being.

Over the years of faithful observance of the Commandments and daily worship, one experiences the progressive stages of Enlightenment. The Commandments, being the *Word* of God, are powerful Polarizers filled with the energy-essences of God's Holy Spirit. The energy-essences of God within the Commandments are the same energy-essences everywhere present throughout the Universe. Polarization attained through worship and the Commandments unites one with the Omnipresent Wisdom and Love of God — therefore, Polarization produces Spiritual Illuminations of increasing breadth, length and height.

Until one begins to work with his soul and with God to attain Polarization, he remains out of harmony with himself, his mate, and with the Cycles of Inheritance. All marital problems, sexual perversions, mental illnesses, emotional disorders and physical-body afflictions are caused by unpolarization. The key to the healing of the sorrows and suffering due to unpolarization is the worship of God and the fulfilling of the Commandments.

The union between the Feminine Polarity and the Masculine Polarity within the human spirit is a mighty endeavor involving all souls on Earth. Marriage, through which male and female are united, is an important aspect of Polarization. The union between man and woman produces children, thereby perpetuating life on Earth.

Through the assistance of the Planets, the Sun and the Moon, a Truth-seeker attains the polarization of his heart and mind. This necessary polarization enables one to give birth to his Divine nature.

The Soul, as a Great Polarizer, determines whether one reincarnates in a male body or a female body. The *Virtues* that the Soul is seeking to bring to birth in one's heart and mind are projections of the Soul's Polarity and Harmony within the Will of God. The birth of Virtues, Conscience, Logic and Love brings one into increasing polarity and harmony with the Soul, the Solar System and the Universe.

As individuals, marriages, nations, races and religions become more Polarized, the human spirit will understand more about Polarization as a Universal Principle affecting all Stars and Galaxies.

TIME: PAST, PRESENT AND FUTURE

Time is holy.

In the 1500's Nicolaus Copernicus revolutionized mankind's concepts of the Solar System. In the 1900's, Albert Einstein revolutionized mankind's concepts of Time and Space. From Einstein, the human spirit has learned:

- Space can be converted to Time, and vice versa.

- Mass can be converted into energy, and vice versa.

- As one travels near the speed of light, Space shrinks; Time expands; and mass increases.

- If one travels at the speed of light, Space shrinks to zero; Time increases to eternity; and one's mass, if he had any in the beginning, increases to Infinity.

The Commandments revealed by Moses and Jesus are great keys or clues to the secrets and mysteries of Time. Each Commandment, if fulfilled with love and reverence, leads one starward and galaxyward. When mankind as a whole embraces the Ten Commandments and the Commandments of Love, the Curtain of the Cosmos will be opened, and the secrets and mysteries of Time, Space and the Universe will no longer be veiled.

Jesus propelled humankind forward on its course toward discovering its innate divinity and eternality. To follow Jesus is to abide by His moral principles and ethical precepts. The Wisdom of Jesus — being eternal and universal in nature — is applicable in any Solar System in the Universe. As one makes the Wisdom of Jesus part of his being, he is initiated into the secrets and mysteries of Time and Timelessness, Space and Spacelessness.

In His victory over death, Jesus prepared the inhabitants of the planet Earth for the time when they would be victorious over death. In His overcoming of Time, Jesus prepared the human spirit to become overcomers of Time.

Time blessed by God is *Time-Grace*. Through Time-Grace, one receives the rewards of the minor and major

Cycles of Inheritance. Time-Grace comes to those who revere Time as a Holy Gift from God.

Time-Grace comes through Time-Polarization. Before one may remain in a continuous State of Grace, he must attain the Polarity-balances within his being and within Time itself.

When one unites with the *Eternal Spirit* of God, he is at one with God as the Past, the Present and the Future. To become polarized within these three aspects of Time enables one to serve God with peace, poise and equanimity. *"Thou wilt keep him in perfect peace, whose mind is stayed on Thee: because he trusteth in Thee." (Isaiah 26:3)*

PROPHECY THROUGH TIME-POLARIZATION

One who knows that God is the Spirit creating Past, Present and Future is able to learn from the Past, past mistakes and past victories; to live ethically and nobly in the Present; and to plant seeds of wisdom and love that will be reaped in the Future.

To think overmuch upon the Past is to become unpolarized as to Time Present and Time Future. To think too much upon the Present is to become unpolarized as to the Past and the Future. To think only upon the Future is to imbalance the Polarization of Time through little regard for the Past and the Present.

To worry continuously about the Future is to burden the physical body, the emotions and the mind. To fear the Future is to find no enjoyment in the Present as a Gift from God. *"Take therefore no thought for the morrow." (St. Matthew 6:34)*

Persons heavily-laden with sin-guilts may reach the time of conscience when they think only of their past offenses against loved ones, self and God. If they remain unrepentant, their dark memories of the Past become a burden—imbalancing the Polarization of Time. However, if such persons truly repent, ask God's forgiveness, make restitution, and resolve to "sin no more" (St. John 5:14), the Polarization of Time is restored. This Gift of God's Mercy and Forgiving Love enables them to be freed from the oppressive burden of sin-memories of the Past, that they may fulfill their spiritual destinies in the Present and prepare for the Divine Marriage in the Future.

Persons totally absorbed in the Present do not realize that their sins of omission and commission will demand payment in the Future. Such persons are ignorant of the karmic Law of Sowing and Reaping. Obsessed with the Present, they gorge themselves on all manner of sin-fruits, unaware of the sicknesses, afflictions and miseries that will be reaped in the Future.

Persons obsessed with thoughts of the Future hoard, connive, manipulate, steal and cheat in order to have comforts and security in the Future. Being miserly and penurious, and driven by a passion to "save" for the Future, they miss life's joys and opportunities in the Present.

Time-Polarization comes during the progressive stages of

union with the Wisdom of God. This Holy Wisdom inspires one to seek to balance the Scales of Divine Justice imbalanced by wrong actions, motives and thoughts in the Past. It also inspires one to observe daily worship of God and daily works of restitution through selfless service to others in the Present. This wholesome attitude toward the Past and the Present polarizes Time as the Scales of Divine Justice come into balance — and the Blessings of the Future become part of the *Now*. In this, one becomes a Time-Polarized Apostle of the Lord Jesus — and the Gifts of Time open as petals of the Lotus of Everlasting Being. The Apostolic Gifts of Healing, Prophecy and Revelation are Time-Gifts that come through Time-Polarization Grace.

Past-lives sins coupled with present-life sins that remain unresolved will present to one a dismal Future. The Future belongs to the pure in heart, the pure in conscience, the pure in soul. *"Blessed are the pure in heart: for they shall see God."* *(St. Matthew 5:8)* Before one can "see" God as the Past, the Present and the Future as *One*, he must become one with the Gifts of Time through the heart-purifications that produce Time-Polarization.

"Worship God: for the testimony of Jesus is the spirit of prophecy." (Revelation 19:10) The prophetic mind is a mind blending Past, Present and Future through Time-Polarization. Blessed is he who serves God with a Time-Polarized Mind. This is the Mind of Christ, the Mind at one with God as the Spirit Eternal beyond Time and Space.

Time-Polarization is the Eternal-Life Consciousness of the Prophet and Apostle anointed, quickened and illuminated by Christ Jesus. The Eternal-Life Consciousness is the Galaxy Consciousness. *"He that receiveth a prophet in the name of a prophet shall receive a prophet's reward." (St. Matthew 10:41)*

THE SPECTRUM OF TIME

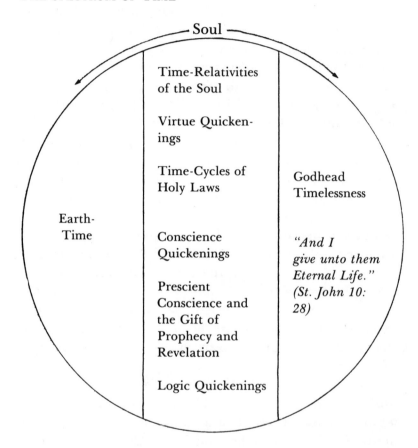

The Spectrum of Time includes Earth-Time, the Time-Relativities of the Soul, and the Timeless Dimensions of the Godhead.

The *Soul* is the means through which Earth-Time is united with Godhead Timelessness. The soul is ever-present in all of one's initiations regarding Time and Timelessness. From the Earth-plane of Time to the Godhead Dimensions of Timelessness—the Eternal Kingdoms of God—the soul's energies are active.

Through reincarnation-cycles directed by the soul's covenant with God, one moves from virtue-initiation to virtue-initiation until he begins to comprehend Time's relationship to Virtue-Births, Virtue-Quickenings and Virtue-Illuminations. Virtue-Illuminations begin one's union with the Glory of God within Timelessness; in this, the Timeless or Eternal Gifts of the soul and the spirit manifest in one's life and being.

In the Parable of the Butterfly, Earth-Time may be likened to the Caterpillar State, for one is *earthbound* in his feelings and thoughts. The Chrysalis State correlates to the virtue-initiations that occur during the probationary period of the higher life. The freedom of the Butterfly symbolizes the Time-Relativity Gifts of the Soul: Remission of Sins, Healing Miracles, Archetypal Prophecies, Revelation-Illuminations, Christ-Mind Quickenings of Grace and Truth.

The degree of one's virtues and conscience determines his relationship with Time. The more one expresses virtues and conscience in service to God, the more he may comprehend God as Universal Creation. Through progressive quickenings of virtues and conscience, a Truth-seeker experiences ever-increasing Time-Relativities until he is firmly united with the Divine Omnipresence within the Spectrum of Time. Union with God's Presence within the Spectrum of Time makes of one a Holy Prophet whose vision may behold the past, the present and the future as revealed by the Creator.

In India, the powerful elephant *Ganesha* of Hindu mythology represents a mighty Attribute of God. Elephant power is awesome, symbolizing the Power of God within His Laws of Creation. To unite with the Ganesha Power through the fulfilling of Holy Law brings forth powers of Prophecy and Revelation; for the Law, when fulfilled, becomes as an elephant clearing away all that stands between one and the Presence of God within Time and Timelessness.

A sin is as a tree in the forest of the Undersoul. Many sins produce a forest thick with a complex tangle of tree branches and undergrowth similar to an impassable jungle area on Earth.

The jungle of sin-trees in the Undersoul obscures one's view of Time's Spectrum — and one is shut away from the dimensional splendor of the soul's eternal light. When one determines to live according to the Commandments of God, the Law becomes as an elephant that tramples down the sin-trees in the jungle of the Undersoul. The removal of the sin-trees enables one to see Time Past and Future as the elephant (law) does its perfect work of clearing away all obstructions. Thus, the fulfilling of God's Law through love gives one the eye of the prophet or seer who sees clearly the Spectrum of Time. The greater the love for God and His Laws, the more extended is one's sight into the Past and the Future.

The Soul may be likened to a space capsule. Wherever one travels between Time and Timelessness, the Soul is present as the vehicle providing the transportation. The virtues present in the heart and mind are quickened degrees of soul-light. Through numerous virtue-quickenings, one progresses from Earth-degrees of Time to Godhead-degrees of Timelessness.

> *Be of good cheer; I have overcome the world.*
> *—St. John 16:33*

TIME-RELATIVITY ZONES

> *Each moment, second, minute and hour consists of energy-units of Time. How one uses these energy-units of Time determines whether he is a sinner or a Saint.*

The Commandments of God are the dividing line between the righteous and the unrighteous, the reverent and the irreverent, the moral and the immoral. The oneness with God attained through the Commandments unites one with the Wisdom and Glory of God within Time.

Sin is the misuse of Time as a God-given energy of Creation. To offend Time by immoral behavior, malicious motives and evil indulgences is to lock one's self in a Time-prison of his own making. This process of self-incarceration is automatic; for the heavy or gross energies within sin place one in a Time-relativity zone devoid of light and grace.

Numerous sins create pockets of Time-energy crystallizations within the physical body, emotions and mind. Wherever these Time-energy crystallizations are located, one experiences various degrees of suffering, affliction, misery, unhappiness. Painful conditions and inharmonious relationships continue until the Time-energy crystallizations caused by one's sins are dissolved through repentance, contrition, confession and restitution.

Sins may be committed on different energy-levels of physical, emotional and mental expression. A sin may begin and end in the mind, or it may move from the mind into the emotional level, gaining momentum until it manifests in the physical world as some hurtful act against oneself or another. The moment one repents of all sin-thoughts, sin-emotions and sin-actions, he has begun to dissolve the Time-energy crystallizations caused by the wrong use of Time.

Sin-thoughts that persist in one's mental-energy processes place one in bondage to mental aberrations, cruel prejudices, lust-obsessions, and spiritual ignorance. Sins committed on the emotional level produce emotional hysterias, nervous breakdowns, and violent offenses against the Commandments of Love. Sins committed on the physical level place one in bondage to selfish pursuits and ungodly habits. The "sins of the flesh" create Time-energy crystallizations that result in physical-body distresses and afflictions.

Through adultery, murder, stealing and other offenses

against the Morality Laws of God, one sets himself back on the Time-Scale. He imprisons himself on the slower-moving tempo of Time's relativity.

The shadows of one's sins may be grey or black. The darker the sins, the slower-moving is Time's energy-processes. As the dark shadows of sin-offenses are forgiven and lightened through God's Mercy and Forgiving Love, a repentant individual is freed from his self-made prison — and he comes into the *energy-currents* of God's Grace within His Commandments. The Commandments-Currents move a sincere penitent into increasing degrees of Divine Grace.

Each degree of God's Grace correlates to a Time-Relativity Zone. As one ascends the Ladder of the Higher Life, he experiences the different Time-Relativity Zones as part of his spiritual education. Eventually, the Commandments-Currents draw the dedicated servant of God into the Archetypal-Grace Flow. The Archetypal-Grace Flow is the goal of all seekers after Truth — for to abide in the Bosom of God's Love is to be in the Archetypal-Grace Flow.

The Anointing Spirit of God is an Eternal, Omnipresent Spirit. To be anointed by God is to be freed from the Time-prisons detaining one's full service to Him. To be "free" in the Biblical meaning of the word is to be free from all bondages.

"If the Son therefore shall make you free, ye shall be free indeed." (St. John 8:36) Jesus, as the Lord of Freedom, is the Door to the freedom of body, heart, mind and soul. To become co-atom to Jesus is to learn of God's Dimensional Grace through which come the progressive states of Enlightenment.

Enlightenment and Freedom are one. Sin leads to bondage; repentance leads to Freedom.

As one progresses spiritually, his relativity to Time changes dramatically. Through sincere repentance and willing restitution, one is *quickened* by the Spirit of God and the Christ.

COMMANDMENTS
OF GOD

The Commandments of Love, Worship, Morality and Giving are the Dividing Line between the Righteous and the Unrighteous. *"If you love me, keep my commandments. (St. John 14:15)*

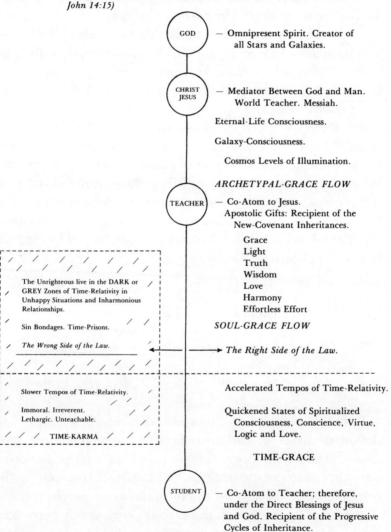

GOD — Omnipresent Spirit. Creator of all Stars and Galaxies.

CHRIST JESUS — Mediator Between God and Man. World Teacher. Messiah.

Eternal-Life Consciousness.

Galaxy-Consciousness.

Cosmos Levels of Illumination.

ARCHETYPAL-GRACE FLOW

TEACHER — Co-Atom to Jesus. Apostolic Gifts: Recipient of the New-Covenant Inheritances.

Grace
Light
Truth
Wisdom
Love
Harmony
Effortless Effort

SOUL-GRACE FLOW

The Unrighteous live in the DARK or GREY Zones of Time-Relativity in Unhappy Situations and Inharmonious Relationships.

Sin Bondages. Time-Prisons.

The Wrong Side of the Law.

The Right Side of the Law.

Slower Tempos of Time-Relativity.

Immoral. Irreverent. Lethargic. Unteachable.

TIME-KARMA

Accelerated Tempos of Time-Relativity.

Quickened States of Spiritualized Consciousness, Conscience, Virtue, Logic and Love.

TIME-GRACE

STUDENT — Co-Atom to Teacher; therefore, under the Direct Blessings of Jesus and God. Recipient of the Progressive Cycles of Inheritance.

TIME-RELATIVITY ZONES

This quickening action lifts one into the Flow of *Soul-Grace*. Through the reverent observance of daily-worship dedications, and unwavering devotion to the Commandments of God, the devotee-initiate expressing Soul-Grace experiences the higher or exalted Time-Relativity Zones.

Anointed servants of God move through their cycles of life within the Flow of *Archetypal Grace*. Therefore, they are able to serve their fellow man, fortified by the Apostolic Time-Grace Gifts of Archetypal Prophecy, Cosmos Revelation, and Dimensional-Healing Powers.

All Time-Cycles in the Universe are part of God's Holy Spirit of Creation. Each Commandment represents the ethical use of Time energy-units on the plane of matter and gravity. When one reveres Time by fulfilling the Commandments in the physical world, he lives in harmony with the Sun, the Moon, the Planets, the Stars and the Galaxies, for their varying Time-Cycles are synchronized in his life and being by God's Holy Spirit of Creation.

DRUGS AND THE DIVINE MARRIAGE

> *Habit-forming drugs on any level are an outrage against Time.*
>
> —*Ann Ree Colton*

In recent decades, millions of individuals have turned to the use of drugs for various reasons. In some instances, persons interested in mystical, religious and spiritual philosophies have turned to the use of drugs as a means of "expanding the consciousness." Drugs are a door to the lower psychic realms of fantasy rather than to the sacred precincts of grace and truth. Such drugs distort one's sense of Time, Space and reality.

In all sacred Scriptures, virtues such as righteousness, self-mastery and love are considered to be the only true route to God-Realization. When the taking of drugs replaces spiritual disciplines, the results are tragic.

Drugs are believed by some to be an easy way to contact God. Those who think that drugs alone will unite them with the Creator are treading a path that leads only to misery and destruction.

Until one loves God with all of his being, as required in the First Commandment, he will fail to qualify for the Divine Marriage. God does not condone a probationer's dependency upon drugs. To tell oneself that one can have God and *also* drug-induced "highs" is to be self-deceived and to move farther and farther away from the Divine-Marriage state of grace.

Drugs do not increase one's sense of morality; in fact, they *decrease* one's sense of morality. Other areas of one's mind, body and being are also seriously affected by drugs. In recent years, medical scientists have learned that marijuana, a popular drug of the times, causes the following conditions:

- Impairment to the brain and nervous system.

- Harm to the lungs, the heart and the immune system.

- Impairment of white blood cells that ordinarily protect the individual from infection.

- Impairing effects on important cells that result in damage to the mind, the personality, the spirit.

- DNA damage. Destruction of chromosomes that pass on genetic instructions to the next generation.

- Disturbed production of protein.

- Damage to sperm cells and ova.

- Damage to nerve and connective-tissue cells.

- Impaired short-term memory.

- Emotional flatness.

- The dropout syndrome: the heavy marijuana user drops out of school, family, religion, etc.

- Diminished will-power.

- Inability to concentrate.

- Short attention span.

- Inability to deal with abstract or complex problems.

- Inability to cope with frustration.

- Increased confusion in thinking.

- Impaired judgment.

- Hostility toward authority.

- Inability to accept the proven medical evidence that marijuana is physically and psychologically harmful.

- Premature senility.

- Regressive immaturity.

> *Marijuana attacks the central nervous system.*
> *Marijuana is an attack on the moral character, on*
> *the integrity.*
>
>   *—Ann Ree Colton*

Drugs destroy the integrity in the consciousness. The consciousness is a priceless gift from God to man. Antichrist works through drugs to remove integrity from the consciousness-mind. If one permits this to occur, he first loses his moral integrity earned after *billions* of years of human-spirit evolution. Then, after the loss of moral, sexual, societal, religious and spiritual integrity, one becomes a destructive force in his own life and in the lives of others. The loss of integrity in the consciousness also reduces the precious energy-units of memory, conscience, will and love. In coming lives, such persons will have to eventually re-earn the integrity in consciousness tragically lost through dependence upon mind-altering drugs.

To serve God, one must be free from any emotional, psychological or physiological dependency upon addictive drugs. To try to live a religious life while addicted to drugs, splits the personality in ever-widening cleavages — and one becomes an agent for the dark.

To meditate while under the influence of mind-altering drugs opens one to the realms of fantasy and entity-possession. Astral gurus expand the ego of drug-takers who are pseudo-students of religion — and keep them bound to their dark and insidious telepathies through the effects of the drug. In this, one keeps in *communion* with the dark and evil entities in the subtle worlds.

The Christ came to bring man freedom through the Sacrament of Communion. The Antichrist seeks to keep man in bondage through the communion with the lower worlds through mind-altering drugs.

Those who take the Sacrament of Communion under Christ and also take drugs under the Antichrist become the tragic victims of their own ignorance, divided loyalties, and lack of discernment of the difference between right and wrong, good and evil.

There is the yin drug-taker and the yang drug-taker. The yin drug-taker, while on the course of self-destruction, does not seek to destroy others. Often, he takes drugs as a form of revenge and hatred against parents, society, or life in general.

On the other hand, the yang drug-taker seeks to involve others in the taking of mind-altering drugs. The yang drug-taker is a menace to himself *and* to others.

In modern times, the casualties of the chemical revolution are mounting each year. Many lives, among them the young and tender in years, are being lost and destroyed. Mental institutions, hospitals, clinics, half-way houses, rehabilitation centers—all are trying to salvage some of the staggering number of individuals who have succumbed to the voice of the Antichrist speaking through drugs, alcohol and other consciousness-destroying chemicals.

The Antichrist comes to destroy. The Christ comes to liberate. The Antichrist seeks to destroy body, heart, mind and soul. Jesus warns His sheep to beware of those who desire to destroy more than the body, but the soul itself. Drugs are one of the ways the Antichrist destroys the body temple, the consciousness-mind, and the soul's record of grace.

The consciousness-mind, when united with the soul and the spirit, opens the Holy of Holies. When God removes the veil from the Holy of Holies, one attains God-Realization. The Antichrist seeks to keep this from happening. The Christ is ever saying: "Come unto me . . . Follow me." One follows the Christ to the Holy of Holies in the consciousness-mind at one with the soul and the spirit.

True followers of Jesus work with the Exorcism Powers of the Lord Christ through the Holy Sacrament. These Exorcism Powers are part of the Crown of Apostleship.

The New-Age Apostle under Christ will be faced increasingly with the problems of others related to drugs such as marijuana, PCP, LSD, cocaine, heroin, etc. More and more will the Apostle-healer under Christ be asked to exorcise the spirit of addiction and the spirit of perversion, companion-evils in modern times.

The healing of individuals, the healing of marriages, the healing of nations, races and religions—all are part of one's

Apostolic service to the Lord of Love. To serve the Lord's
Communion is a sacred opportunity to seal His Love and
Light more deeply into the hearts and minds of those who
seek to unite with God in the Marriage Divine.

> *Only persons centered in God can serve God. All*
> *forms of illusory addiction interfere with centering.*
> *A centered person draws to him those who are also*
> *centered. From this is the reinforcement whereby*
> *a perfected polarization becomes the vehicle for the*
> *God-Presence.*
>
> *—Ann Ree Colton*

PRAYER OF HEALING FOR FORMER DRUG-TAKERS

Aspirants of the spiritual life who used drugs in the past
should speak prayers of repentance and fulfill works of restitution. In this, they will rectify former abuses of the Body
Temple and offenses against the Divine Image.

> *Dear Lord, please forgive me for offending the*
> *Body Temple and the Divine Image. Help me to*
> *regain my self-worth as a child of Thy Pure and*
> *Holy Spirit. Bless all persons I may have influenced*
> *to turn toward drugs rather than toward Thy Prin-*
> *ciples of Righteousness and Love.*
> *May all Scales of Thy Justice come into balance,*
> *that I may serve Thee with a whole heart, mind,*
> *soul and spirit.*
> *In Jesus' Holy Name.*
> *Amen.*

Students on the Path who turned toward drugs earlier in
their lives should be ever alert to the voice of the tester seeking to lure them into the *drugged state* of procrastination and
unpunctuality. The concerted effort by a student to work with

his Teacher in the overcoming of these undesirable and dangerous traits will manifest a great victory in the soul's record—and the joy of being in timing with God and His Plan will bless the student in this life and in coming lives.

If a student who was a former drug-taker continues to respond to the voice of the tester, he will miss key timings and Grace-Inheritances due to procrastination and unpunctuality. In this, the tester will be as effective and deadly in the student's spiritual life as in his drug-taking days. Also, a new danger is added—for the student's closeness to an Anointed Teacher places the student in a position to be used by the Antichrist to interfere with the Christ Dharma blessing the world through the Teacher and the Teaching.

PUNCTUALITY AND THE HIERARCHS

God is Eternal Punctuality.

Self-mastery begins the process of the mastery of Time. Self-discipline and self-control are essential for self-mastery. Self-mastery is necessary for Self-Realization. Self-Realization is necessary for God-Realization. Thus, God-Realization begins with self-discipline.

Unpunctuality reveals a need for self-discipline. One who flows with the grace-currents of Time moves in harmony with God's precise, orderly Creation of the Universe.

An habitually unpunctual person is a sin-laden individual who has lost touch with God as Time, God as Truth, God as Love. To come under the Christ is to come into Perfect Timing with God's Dimensional Spirit within Time and Timelessness.

Chronic unpunctuality as an offense against Time may begin to be corrected through sincere apology to God and man. Every time a Truth-seeker is unpunctual, he moves farther away from Truth. Every time he fails to apologize to God and to those whom he has inconvenienced, he has moved farther away from good manners.

If one cannot apologize to a fellow human being, he cannot confess to God. Apology overcomes the Time-factor. Confession overcomes the Time-factor.

The Christ and the Hierarchs working with God in the creation of Solar Systems utilize the Principle and Virtue of Punctuality as one of the major factors in Pure Creation. Their use of the Principle and Virtue of Punctuality may be likened to members of an orchestra playing in perfect synchronization and harmony.

When a devotee of the higher life begins to realize the importance of Punctuality, he is being inspired by his soul, the Christ and the Hierarchs. Gradually, he will come into perfect union with the Wisdom and Glory of God within the Virtue of Punctuality. In this, he becomes enlightened as to Time and Timing and their relationship to Pure Creation, the Divine Image, the Constellation Energies, the Seasonal Cycles, the Solar, Lunar and Planetary Energy-Harmonics, and other Cosmic and Cosmos Truths.

The Hierarchs and the Christ, the Angels and the Archangels work through Planetary Punctuality. To revere Time and to come into timing with Planetary Punctuality brings understanding through union with the Wisdom of God creating Time and the Planets.

The Christ is punctual in all blessings, healings, anointings, sealings and quickenings. To come under the Christ is to come into Perfect Timing with the flows of Soul-Grace and Divine Grace. Dedicated punctuality keeps one united with the precision of God in His creation of the Planets, the Moon, the Sun, the Stars and the Galaxies.

The Christ is between God and man; the Hierarchs are between Christ and man. The devotee first becomes a protege of the Saints who assist him to bring forth the virtues to be used in service to God. With the birth of the virtues, the devotee also becomes a protege of the Hierarchs. When one becomes a protege of the Hierarchs, he then may work directly with the Christ and God, for he has attained a high degree of divine union.

The Teacher's work is to inspire each student to express all virtues in service to God. Students who respond to this instruction come under the blessed assistance of the Angels and the Saints. The Teacher works with responsive students on the higher levels of knowledge, dedication, and service to God.

A reverent and conscientious student expresses the *sacrament-degrees* of the virtues—that is, all virtues are used in sacramental service to God. The sacrament-degrees of the virtues are one's first glimpse of the Glory of God within the Soul and the Divine Image. Thereafter, the Teacher may work with the student on even higher levels of instruction, service and pure creation.

Through the sacrament-degrees of the virtues, a student becomes a protege of the Hierarchs who work directly with and through his constancy, punctuality and other sanctified virtues. In this, the student becomes an anointed one united with the Grace of Revelation. The Grace of Revelation denotes that one has begun his hierarchy work for God, for he is at one with the Hierarchs, the Christ and the Creator.

Is it not written in your law, I said, Ye are gods?
—St. John 10:34

The Healing of Procrastination

A procrastinator simply cannot flow with the Cycles. Procrastination is death to God's Increase.
—Ann Ree Colton

Procrastination and unpunctuality are major offenses against Time-Polarization. If these faults are present in one's nature, they hinder his coming into timing with the harmony of the Solar-System Time-Cycles.

Each cyclic Inheritance of Grace is a manifestation of God's precious elixirs and essences. To claim one's spiritual birthright of cyclic Inheritances of Grace requires that he move with the tide of instruction being presented by his Living Teacher. One forfeits this Grace through procrastination; one inherits this Grace through diligence, conscientiousness and gratitude.

Procrastination caused by unevolved virtues and unresolved sins of the present life and past lives acts as a drug upon the mind and the body, thereby nullifying incentive and enthusiasm. Without incentive and enthusiasm, one remains spiritually unawakened.

As one repents of his sins, the drug-like effect of procrastination begins to disappear—and one experiences his first spiritual awakenings and soul-grace quickenings. These, in turn, produce incentive and enthusiasm. Incentive keeps one centered in God's Grace and enthusiasm keeps him centered in God's Love.

Incentive inspires one to keep trying regardless of the adversities and challenges on the Path. Enthusiasm enables him to transcend the levels of life occupied by the apathetic, the lethargic, the complacent, and all others under the spell of the hypnotic drug of procrastination.

Sins create heavy energies. These heavy energies short-circuit the electricities of the mind, the body and the soul. Thus, repetitive sins result in blockages between the spirit and the body, the soul and the mind.

Without spirit and soul, the body becomes lazy; the mind, uninspired. With incentive and enthusiasm, the body becomes buoyant; the mind is filled with thoughts inspired by the soul and the spirit.

He who has incentive has motivation; procrastination negates motivation.

Enthusiasm is expressed by all enlightened servants of God, for they are *energized* by the Spirit of God. To be energized by the Spirit of God is to serve Him each day with holy enthusiasm.

Incentive leads one Godward. Enthusiasm makes even the most difficult tasks a joy.

Without incentive, man perishes. With incentive, the soul soars.

Without enthusiasm, man sinks into sin-fixities. Incentive and enthusiasm explode the sin-fixities, thereby liberating the grace-energies of the soul and the spirit.

The Bible is a Book of Incentive. The Bible is a Book of Enthusiasm. The Spirit of God leaps forth from the pages of the Bible to awaken one from the drug-like sleep of procrastination. Incentive leads one to the Light; Enthusiasm makes the journey a happy one.

> *In order to do great things, one must be enthusiastic.*
>
> —*St. Simon*

The *Great Procrastination* is to wait until a coming life before one turns to God as a sincere worshipper, a reverent doer of His Word, and an obedient student of a Living Teacher. Individuals who are victims of the Great Procrastination lose much ground in their present life and subject themselves to strong reprovings from their souls in future lives. In each life, one is given the opportunity to move closer to God or to move farther away from Him.

Some persons are blessed with freedom of time, financial security, and a Living Teacher. However, if they are not alert, they will sell their spiritual birthrights for a mess of pottage — the pottage of procrastination. Individuals who receive their spiritual birthrights in their present lifetimes experience the Love, Grace and Truth of God in increasing measures.

Many students of the higher life believe themselves to be paragons of virtue when, in reality, they are paragons of procrastination. God's Spirit abides not in the atmosphere of procrastination. His Spirit comes only where there is reverence for His Gift of Time.

To be in timing with God is to be in timing with the Clock of Cosmos. Miraculous *coincidings* come to those who love Time as a Gift of God.

Persons who enjoy doing all things promptly and paying all bills quickly will inherit in future lives the virtues related to Perfect Timing. This virtue-grace is a rich treasure one bequeaths to himself from life to life. *"But lay up for yourselves treasures in heaven . . ." (St. Matthew 6:20)*

To marry a procrastinator is to marry an unwell person afflicted with a disease similar to sleeping sickness. Procrastinators, though physically awake, are spiritually asleep to the vitality of Soul-Life, the beauty of Time, and the harmony of Creation.

The *desire* to be healed of procrastination begins one's linking with the Miracle-Light of the Christ. The healing of procrastination is the equivalent of being raised from the dead—for each is a spiritual-quickening miracle!

PRAYER FOR THE HEALING OF PROCRASTINATION

Heal me of procrastination, O Lord, that I may do Thy Will.
Heal me, that I may move with the Tide of Thy Love.
Heal me, that I may heal others in Jesus' Name.
Amen.

RECTIFICATION PRAYER: TO BECOME AWARE OF GOD'S FACE WITHIN TIME

Dear Lord, I confess my sins regarding the wrong use of Thy precious Gift of Time. I pray to make a full and honorable restitution for all sins committed in the present life and in past lives: sins of unpunctuality, procrastination and other thoughtless, careless and selfish acts. Please forgive me, I pray—and bless all whom I have offended in the present life and in past lives.

May all scales come into balance, and may all threads become untangled—that I may see Thee with clear sight and serve Thee with clean hands and a pure heart.

Blessed art Thou, O Lord. I pray to become one with Thee. May I see Thy Face within Time, that I may better serve Thee as a steward of Thy mysteries, a protector and preserver of Thy Dharma, a revealer of Thy Word and Plan.
                In Jesus' Name.
                Amen.

Unpunctuality, procrastination, the irreverent use of Time, the squandering of Time, the usurping of other persons' Time, and all other offenses against Time are mercifully forgiven and healed by God as one changes his attitudes toward Time, reveres Time, and prays to henceforth receive God's help, wisdom and blessings in his future use of Time. Prayers in which one expresses the heartfelt desire to make rectification for sins against Time committed in his present life and past lives, will result in realizations and inspirations regarding the sacredness of Time and the divine purposes of Time as a Gift from God.

"When thou saidst, Seek ye my face; my heart said unto thee, thy face, Lord, will I seek." (Psalm 27:8) Prayers of confession accompanied by sacrificial acts of rectification, restitution-fasts and atonement-offerings remove many motes from the eyes until one may see clearly the Face of God within Time. The reverent, disciplined and sacramental use of Time qualifies one to receive the gifts of the soul and the spirit. Thereafter, his prayers and meditations become natural expressions of the royal gifts of Healing, Prophecy and Revelation. These mighty gifts denote that the Truth-seeker has made union with the Glory of God within Time.

The higher life begins with repentance and prospers with restitution. When one desires to make a full and honorable restitution for all offenses, sins and transgressions of the present life and past lives, God rewards this noble desire in countless ways. Gradually, Time becomes polarized within one's life and being through increasing words and acts of restitution.

The more freedom one experiences through restitution, the more he desires to teach, heal and inspire others. This desire accelerates the Restitution Process through which comes union with Time-Polarization Grace.

When Jesus healed the ten lepers in the twinkling of an eye, He utilized His knowledge of Time to change their misery into joy. Each time one teaches others in the Name of the Christ, the seeds of Truth planted in their hearts and minds are filled with the healing-essences of the Christ. These are the same healing-essences that freed the lepers from their affliction, lifting them from sorrow to happiness in a moment of Time.

God's Omnipresence beyond Time and Space blesses the Teacher of His sacred truths in many miraculous ways. When one teaches sacramentally as an Apostle of the Christ, he is sealing into the soul-memories of Truth-seekers the living, vital and volatile seeds of Grace and Truth. These seeds will remain within the memory cells of the hearers during their present lives and all future lives. The Teacher receives the *eternal blessings* of God for sealing *eternal truths* into the hearts and minds of His children. This mighty manifestation of God's gratitude frees the Teacher to greater ranges of realization and revelation.

The benefits to be gained by those who are receiving the Teacher's instruction — benefits blessing their present life and future lives — are applied to the Teacher's present state of Restitution. God as Past, Present and Future knows exactly how each of His children will be blessed by the Teacher's instruction in all of their lives to come — and credits the Teacher in the *Now* for these benefits. Thus, when one teaches Holy Laws, Sacred Principles, Divine Virtues and Christ-Ethics to others, he rapidly resolves his own past-lives' indebtedness — and he realizes God's Sweet Mercy and Freedom-Anointings in the present.

To overcome karma is to overcome Time. Love overcomes karma; Love overcomes Time. *"Walk in wisdom toward them that are without, redeeming the time." (Colossians 4:5)*

God says: I am Time.
O *worshipper, learn to see My Face in*
  Time,
and I will reveal My Face to thee.
Live each day
according to My Way.
And I will also reveal to thee
My Face in Eternity, Infinity, Eternality.

The Timeless One am I.
I dwell in all regions of Time
and in all reaches of Timelessness.

Behold My Countenance
smiling upon thee from the Cosmos.
Receive My Smile
through thy reverence for Time.
Make Time thy friend,
and I am there to guide thee
and to establish thee in Truth.

Time and Truth are inseparable.
Time is Truth,
and Truth is Time.
I am Truth,
and I am Time.

Follow My Eternal Son
Along the Spectrum-Path of Holy Time.
He will shepherd thee
to the Bosom of My Love
wherein may be found
the secret treasures of Time
and the keys to all doors of Truth.

I am Time.
Past, Present and Future am I.
Ascend the Hill of Holiness,
that thine eyes may perceive
all directions of Time.
The higher thou dost climb the Hill of
    Holiness,
the farther wilt thou see Time past and
    Time future.

Become thou a prophet who proclaims My
    Glory within Time.

And My Spirit will be upon thee—
the Spirit that is Time,
the Spirit that is beyond Time.

My Will decreeth;
My Image quickeneth;
My Plan fulfilleth.
Through Time, thou learnest of My Will,
    Image and Plan.

Stand as a Timeless one within Time.
To unite with Me is to become
a Timeless one within Time.
To be a Timeless one within Time
is to be in Perfect Timing with all that is
and with all that shall ever be.

BIBLIOGRAPHY

Abell, George, *Exploration of the Universe*, Holt, Rinehart and Winston, Inc., New York, 1973.

Berman, Louis, *Exploring the Cosmos*, Little, Brown and Co., Boston, 1973.

Cornell, James and Hayes, E. Nelson, Editors, *Man and Cosmos*, W. W. Norton and Company, Inc., New York, 1975.

Darling, David, "The Quasar Connections," *Astronomy*, December 1979.

Dobin, Joel C., *To Rule Both Day and Night*, Inner Traditions International, New York, 1977.

Edwards, Betty, *Drawing on the Right Side of the Brain*, J. P. Tarcher, Inc., Distributed by Houghton Mifflin Co., Boston, 1979.

Elders, Lee J.; Nilsson-Elders, Brit; Welch, Thomas K.; *UFO . . . Contact From the Pleiades*, Volume 1, Genesis III Productions, Ltd., Phoenix, Arizona, 1979.

Ferris, Timothy, *Galaxies*, Sierra Club Books, San Francisco, 1980.

Goldstein, Philip, *Genetics is Easy*, Lantern, Mt. Vernon, New York, 1967.

Holy Bible, King James Version.

Jastrow, Robert, *God and the Astronomers*, W. W. Norton and Company, Inc., New York, 1978.

Sarnoff, Jane and Ruffins, Reynold, *Space: A Fact and Riddle Book*, Charles Scribner's Sons, New York, 1978.

Shields, Gregory, "The Chemistry of Galaxies," *Astronomy*, June 1981.

Woods, Ralph, Editor and Compiler, *The World Treasury of Religious Quotations*, Hawthorn Books, Inc., New York, 1966.

Zeilik, Michael, *Astronomy: The Evolving Universe*, Harper and Row, New York, 1976.

INDEX

Inclusive of Quotation References

OTHER BOOKS BY ANN REE COLTON

THE THIRD MUSIC
A powerful book describing the energy-worlds of the Mind, the Soul, and the Universe.

KUNDALINI WEST
Knowledge of the Kundalini and the Chakras for the Western initiate.

WATCH YOUR DREAMS
An invaluable and necessary book revealing the soul-codes in dreams and their symbols.

ETHICAL ESP
An important book defining the difference between lower and higher ESP.

THE JESUS STORY
A miracle book in timing to the need for miracles.

THE HUMAN SPIRIT
A scientific, spiritual, and healing book on the creation, purpose and destiny of man.

PROPHET FOR THE ARCHANGELS
The life story of Ann Ree Colton. (Co-Author, Jonathan Murro)

THE SOUL AND THE ETHIC
A profound book on the soul and on the ethical use of soul-power.

THE KING
From the personal, hieroglyphic journal of Ann Ree Colton.

DRAUGHTS OF REMEMBRANCE
An extraordinary book on the subject of reincarnation.

MEN IN WHITE APPAREL
A book of vital revelations about death and the life after death.

THE VENERABLE ONE
An initiatory book for those who love Nature and who would unveil Nature's secrets.

VISION FOR THE FUTURE
A prophetic book to comfort men in a perilous time.

THE LIVELY ORACLES
A prophetic book on world events.

ISLANDS OF LIGHT
A book of initiation with an underlying prophetic theme.

PRECEPTS FOR THE YOUNG
Appreciated by the adult . . . inspiring to the child . . . beneficial to the family.

BOOKS BY JONATHAN MURRO

THE PATH OF VIRTUE
A comprehensive work that describes the classic route to Enlighten-ment traveled by all Great Souls of the East and the West.

GOD-REALIZATION JOURNAL
A book opening a new world of understanding related to the Presence of God. *God-Realization Journal* also describes the author's initiatory transition from a devotee to a teacher of the higher life.

ANN REE COLTON FOUNDATION
P.O. Box 2057   Glendale, California 91209

ABOUT THE AUTHORS

Ann Ree Colton, with the assistance of Jonathan Murro, her husband and co-worker, has produced a System of Enlightenment for those who seek a positive and pure method of procedure on the Path. This System, called *Niscience*, means Knowing. When one enters the instruction of Niscience, he comes into the Archetypal Path; he quickens the gifts of his soul and experiences within his own higher mind the Archetypal Insights.

For many years, Ann Ree Colton has experienced the revelatory state of grace connecting the soul with the Cosmic and Cosmos. Through the Archetypal Light, her initiatory processes have been expressed as books, lectures, teaching, and methods of healing. Each of her books progressively leads the reader into the mind-dharma, where he encounters God through realization and illumination.

Jonathan Murro is the author of *God-Realization Journal, The Path of Virtue* and co-author of *Prophet for the Archangels*, the life-story of Ann Ree Colton.